Politicians Above The Law
Comments received to date
Feb 6, 2011

* * *

During my twenty-one years in the Canadian House of Commons, three of them as Government House Leader, I participated in many discussions and debates about the rights and privileges of Members of Parliament. During this time , if there were books like <u>Politicians Above The Law</u>, which presents a scholarly and analytic assessment of some of those rights and privileges, I was unaware of them. Thus in writing this book, Maingot and Dehler not only present a strong argument for the abolition of parliamentary inviolability, but also contribute to a rather sparse body of work on the important area of how parliamentarians should govern themselves.

Hon. Harvie Andre,
Calgary, Alberta . Canada

* * *

Parliamentary immunity is a necessary guarantee of the independence of the legislature. When it extends to protecting members beyond their parliamentary activities from the criminal justice system however, it brings the legislature into disrepute and there can be few greater attacks on its independence than that caused by the contempt this engenders. You may not agree with every point made by Joseph Maingot but I believe you will agree this book should be read.

The Right Honourable Paul Martin,
former Prime Minister of Canada

* * *

The author of <u>Politicians Above The Law</u> presents a most compelling case for the abolition of parliamentary inviolability as contrasted with the necessary concept of parliamentary immunity. Any truly democratic society requires that a member of any legislative body should be accountable to the criminal justice system.

Hon. R. Roy McMurtry,
former Canadian High Commissioer to London,
former Attorney General of the Province of Ontatio,
and former Chief Justice of the Province of Ontario

* * *

In <u>Politicians Above The Law</u>, Maingot points out that democracy must distinguish between parliamentary immunity and parliamentary inviolability. The former, the right to speak freely in Parliament is desirable. The latter, exempting elected officials from the Criminal Code, is not. What is most disturbing is Maingot's revealing evidence that in many of the world's democracies, it is legal inviolability that prevails. Maingot calls passionately for this to change.

Hon. Ed Broadbent,
first President of the International Centre for
Human Rights and Democratic Development,
and former national leader of the
New Democratic Party of Canada

POLITICIANS ABOVE THE LAW

A case for the abolition of parliamentary inviolability

[signature]

J.P. JOSEPH MAINGOT Q.C.
WITH DAVID DEHLER Q.C.

POLITICIANS ABOVE THE LAW
Copyright © 2010 by J.P. Joseph Maingot

ISBN: 978-1-926596-84-6

Published by:

Baico Publishing Inc.
294 Albert Street, Suite 103
Ottawa, Ontario K1P 6E6
Tel: (613) 829-5141
E-mail: baico@bellnet.ca
Visit Baico Website at: www.baico.ca

Printed by Document Majemta Inc.

POLITICIANS
ABOVE THE LAW

A case for the abolition
of parliamentary inviolability

In October 2009, the June 18, 2003 law which shielded the Prime Minister (Berlusconi), the speakers of the two houses and the head of the constitutional court, was ruled unconstitutional by Italy's Constitutional court, as it breached the Article of the Constitution making all citizens equal before the law. One of Mr. Berlusconi's lawyers had argued that he is no longer 'first among equals', but ought to be considered 'First above equals'.

*Rome, 9 October, 2009, The Globe and Mail

Legislation may not change the heart
but it may restrain the heartless.

List of Contents

À Simone

PREFACE

The genesis of this book springs from the three months I spent in East Timor as one of the constitutional consultants offered by the Inter-Parliamentary Union to the newly elected Constituent Assembly. I had arrived in Dili, the capital, just days before the infamous event of September 11, 2001.

When the subject of parliamentary immunity arose during our deliberations, I pointed out the differences between the Westminster model and elsewhere. I recall telling the members of the relevant committee of the Assembly that news reports from the Russian Federation, whose Duma provides inviolability to its members, were saying in 1998 that "a growing number of Russian criminals are seeking elected office to gain immunity from prosecution". (see Chapter 6). Thoughts then germinated and multiplied. Slowly the book began to take shape.

In early 2005, I completed a rough first draft. Two critiques of that draft provided the impetus to stay the course with greater effort, more research and better organization. The objective now was to try and produce something informative for the interested general public and yet sufficiently scholarly to serve possibly as a handy international reference work for academics, journalists, parliamentarians, and jurists.

The manuscript required constant revisions with further research and information and the work was intermittent. The very helpful assistance from many members of the reference branch of the Canadian Library of Parliament was truly exceptional. They brought to my attention international authors who had dealt with various aspects of this elusive and little known area of parliamentary law, practice and procedure, and relevant news reports from around the world. I am very grateful to them for their generous help.

The word perfect process involved considerable work. Early in 2004 my wonderful and bright step granddaughter, Kateri Couture-Latour, then only 14 years of age, started this work and continued loyally, faithfully and expertly, until she became too busy pursuing two majors in university.

However my warmest thanks go to my very dear friend David Dehler, Q.C., M.A., LL.B, L.Ph, LL.L. David had assisted me with Chapter 14 of my second edition of <u>Parliamentary Privilege in Canada</u>, 1997 dealing as it did with the effect of the Canadian Charter of Rights and Freedoms on parliamentary privilege. Here, in this present book, his collaboration over many months of discussions and revisions following upon the third party critiques of the rough first draft, was outstanding and again I owe him a special debt of gratitude, in particular for the concluding chapter. Our many discussions, his questions, revisions and ongoing encouragement throughout were essential to bring my book to conclusion. Indeed the final chapter reflects majorly his musings down the years in various other contexts of political thought, law, human rights, and the human yearning for meaning and truth which I happily share and endorse in the present context of the overall thrust of my book.

Introduction:
Parliamentary Immunity Versus
Parliamentary Inviolability

Most people would probably agree that a member of parliament or of a national assembly should enjoy immunity while in parliament or the national assembly. The question then arises, what should be the extent of such parliamentary immunity and should it extend beyond the precincts of parliament or the assembly?

This book argues that no member of any national legislative body across the globe should enjoy special immunity from the criminal justice system.

The reader may ask, do they? The answer is yes, many do. More than 70% of the world's nations spell out clearly in their constitutions or in legislation that members of their parliaments or national assemblies are protected from the criminal process in various ways: they may not be prosecuted, or detained, or arrested without prior consent of the parliament or the assembly in which they sit. This is called parliamentary inviolability.

Only the Commonwealth parliaments and the Congress of the United States of America refuse to grant such special immunity to their members. Rampant worldwide, however, is such special immunity from the criminal justice system which is referred to throughout as parliamentary inviolability to distinguish it from parliamentary immunity.

The latter refers to an exemption from some of the laws of a country that is deemed necessary to permit parliamentarians to perform their parliamentary functions and to get to and from parliament and their constituency. Parliamentary immunity refers throughout to the historically developed immunities of a member of parliament deemed necessary to get on with the work of parliament and good governance: freedom of speech in parliament, and protection when traveling to and from parliament. This excludes parliamentary inviolability.

Today, transparency in financial affairs, whether of governments, the United Nations, or the private sector, and accountability to stakeholders, attract a great deal of commentary. But the issue of parliamentary inviolability draws little systematic study. There are indeed many press reports on its uses and abuses. The press reports ensure that parliamentary inviolability is transparent. The constitutional texts ensure that accountability for alleged criminal activity shall not be demanded.

This gives rise to a degree of cynicism, and some reports even go so far as to allege that some persons in some countries enter politics to protect themselves from the criminal justice system. Consider three examples from three different countries: Italy, Russia, and Guatemala.

The Italian example concerns Silvio Berlusconi. In 2004, Parliamentary Affairs reported that he was "under investigation for a variety of crimes... (hence the rumours that he had entered politics in order to try to protect himself from the judiciary)."[1] Previously, in 2003, reporting on proposed Italian legislation to protect from prosecution not only Prime Minister

Berlusconi but also the President of the Republic and the Speakers of both Houses of Parliament, The Guardian wrote that an Italian senator had said, "It is not a scandal to discuss parliamentary immunity… What is scandalous is to think that immunity becomes impunity… People [getting] elected not to serve their country but to avoid being prosecuted."[2]

In 1995, the Globe and Mail reported that the Russian Parliament was "facing a flood of new candidates with criminal records who are scrambling to get elected so they can enjoy immunity from prosecution."* In 2004, the Latin America Weekly Report stated that former president Alfonso Portillo of Guatemala had used his prerogative of ex officio member of Parlecan (Regional Parliament of Central America) "to shield himself from prosecution on corruptions charges."[3]

Offsetting possible political cynicism in Italy was the good news that the proposed legislation was declared "illegitimate" by Italy's Constitution Court because it violated the constitutionally enshrined principle that all citizens are equal before the law.[4]

The reader should keep in mind throughout that parliamentary immunity is not a member's personal privilege but a guarantee of the independence of parliament and its members in relation to other authorities. It should be primarily a sanctuary that provides for freedom of speech and the freedom to act while taking part in a proceeding of parliament. The Speaker of the Canadian House of Commons put it succinctly in 1971:[5]

> In my view, parliamentary privilege (immunity) does not go much beyond the right of free speech in the

---

* Globe and Mail, 7 October 1995. Plus ça change… Also see Russian Court says there's enough evidence to lift immunity of deputy in hotel fraud case", Globe and Mail, Feb. 20, 2002. For an update on the Kremlin entitled Why Kremlin v. Khodorkovsky still matters, see Amy Knight, Globe & Mail, Feb. 9, 2007.

House of Commons and the right of a Member to discharge his duties in the House as a Member of the House of Commons.

In sum, parliamentary immunity is a fundamental right necessary for the exercise of the constitutional function of parliament and of the person elected to a parliament. Its principal application is to anything a member of parliament may say or do within the scope of his or her duties in the course of parliamentary business. It also extends to permit the member to attend parliamentary business in parliament unimpeded, and to protect the member beyond the walls of parliament for what he says or does during a proceeding in parliament. A member of parliament is elected to represent constituents through service in parliament or the national assembly. As a country's most important public body, parliament has first call on the services of its members.

This is an ancient concept. This immunity applied originally to all assemblies including the plebeian tribunes of Rome. It continued with the Althingi in Iceland in the tenth century and with the earliest assemblies in England gathered to advise the Crown. As early as 287 B.C., the comitia tribune (assembly of all the people – plebeians and patricians alike) was given the power to make laws that bound everyone. Tribunes and the comitia remained to protect the poor classes of Rome until the end of the Republic in 27 B.C. The immunity speaks of the inviolability of the persons of the tribunes as holy and sacrosanct and who therefore could not be imprisoned. The tribunes could punish infringement of their inviolability by various punishments up to throwing the offender – even if he were a magistrate – off the Tarpeian Rock.[6] Ours is not the day of the Roman tribunes though it appears that many politicians worldwide seem to think they should enjoy a like inviolability.

Iceland alone housed for centuries a Christian literate society with no prince of any kind and no unified executive power. It offers a rare example of a society that tried to preserve law and order without a ruler. Whether this was a remnant of a world lost elsewhere or a new development is not certain. Iceland was then (tenth century) governed by chieftains, a system of balance that was simultaneously fragile. The Althingi was the assembly of the country's most powerful chieftains. All freemen were entitled to attend the Althingi, which was held in 930 A.D. Within the sanctuary of the Althingi, all were entitled to truce and the freedom to follow proceedings. This was basically just one of the things which Germanic peoples had held from time immemorial. The main concern while at the Althingi was not to be killed of maimed. Leave your weapons at the door! At Thingvellir, members of the Althingi had their quarters where they resided for the duration of the assembly.[*]

The Constitution of Iceland, now provides under Article 49:

"No Member of Althingi may be subjected to custody on remand during a session of Althingi without the permission of Althingi, nor may a criminal action be brought against him unless he is caught in the act of committing a crime.

---

[*] The History of Iceland. Gunnar Karlsson: University of Minnesota Press, Minneapolis, 2000. Wherever Norsemen settled they established a regular assembly, which was commonly called Althingi, the assembly of all free males, perhaps of some minimal social status. There is no reason to assume that the constitution of Iceland was in the beginning very different from any Norse – or Germanic – governing system in the centuries preceding the Viking Age. The Roman author Tacitus describes a Germani 'thing' around 100 A.D.

No Member of Althingi may be made responsible outside Althingi for statements made by him in Althingi, except with the permission of Althingi."

The question that persists may be asked in different ways. Why should modern-day politicians anywhere in the world enjoy parliamentary inviolability? How can this be reconciled with the rule of law, good governance, and equality before the law? Was the Constitution Court of Italy not correct in adjudging that the proposed legislation contradicted the principle of equality before the law? Why should a member of any legislative body not be accountable to the criminal justice system for what he or she does beyond Parliament like everyone else? How did parliamentary inviolability arise? When will it end? How can we end it?

These pages, then attempt in a systematic way to bring to the attention of the general reader the disturbing reality worldwide of parliamentary inviolability. Chapter 1 explains the role of a modern-day constitution and the history and politics of the "rule of law". Chapter 2 explores the British parliamentary experience and its Canadian offshoot to show, from an historical perspective, how and why parliamentary immunity never included parliamentary inviolability. Chapter 3 uses the same historical perspective to explain how and why parliamentary inviolability arose in the parliaments of continental Europe and beyond, contrary to the British experience. Chapter 4 examines parliamentary inviolability in the European Parliament. Chapter 5 asks and answers very briefly the question, why is a member of parliament elected; and it serves to sum up what came before and to set the stage for the critical assessment of parliamentary inviolability and the consideration of its elimination. Chapter 6 reviews the concrete reality of parliamentary inviolability. The concluding Chapter 7 invites the European Parliament to lead the way in abolishing the repugnant claim to parliamentary inviolability and thereby provide transparent evidence of a genuine desire to promote good governance, equality before the law and the rule of law. The abolition of parliamentary inviolability across the world is an urgent priority in all discussions, policies, and practices aimed at promoting these goals.

This book therefore invites debate and constructive criticism. It is only a prod to further and deeper systematic study and action. It does not claim in any way to offer a blueprint that, if followed, will bring about planetary peace and goodwill. It does, however, make the modest claim that the abolition of parliamentary inviolability worldwide must be an urgent priority to advance good governance, equality before the law, the rule of law, human rights and yes, peace in the world. It is a needed start to combatting corruption in some high places. Making the abolition of parliamentary inviolability a priority constitutes an essential contribution to all projects relating to good governance. In the words of a professor at the university of Vienna, Christian Kopetzki, writing about parliamentary inviolability (which he refers to as immunity):

> The general public has an ambivalent attitude toward the immunity of its elected representatives in an age when the reduction of privilege is ostensibly the order of the day. While the proponents of parliamentary immunity defend it as "the last bastion of the constitution," its critics speak of a "sickness of the political system," the abolition of which is an urgent matter of "political hygiene."[7]

I hope to help chip away at the encrusted sophistic prejudice that presumes parliamentary inviolability must be retained as "the last bastion of the constitution," or otherwise. Rather than a bastion of the constitution, it weighs heavily as a burden on the body politic and constitutes a grave impediment to the growth of good governance, the rule of law, and equality before the law worldwide.

Chapter 1
What a Modern Constitution
Does and the Rule of Law

A constitution grounds the legal framework of a political society. According to Charles McIlwain, author of Constitutionalism: Ancient and Modern, the modern sense of the word constitution denotes "the whole legal framework of the state." McIlwain adds, "It would require a very detailed examination of the legal and political writings of several centuries to enable one to say with any confidence when this modern conception of a constitution first appears."*

For practical purposes, we can agree with David Beatty, author of Constitutional Law in Theory and Practice, that "constitutions… are universally understood to be all about governments, what institutions they include, how they are structured, and what kind of power they can wield."[8]

Further, as Beatty explains, "[t]ypically, in liberal democratic societies at least, constitutions impose four broad conditions – or constraints – on how the power of a state can be exercised."[9] They are: (1) the principle of democratic, or popular, vote; (2) the idea of separation of powers; (3) territorial division in a federation according to a federal principle; and (4) absolute

---

* Charles Howard McIlwain, Constitutionalism: Ancient and Modern, Cornell Paperbacks, Cornell University Press, Ithaca and London, Revised Edition, 1947, p. 24. Professor McIlwain's guess is that the opening of the seventeenth century provides the first clear instance of its modern usage.

| 1

limits on what the state or any of its officials may do. In this last regard, Beatty states:[10]

> Almost every constitution that has been written since the end of the Second World War contains a long list of basic human rights which no government is permitted to transgress. Fundamental freedoms of religion, expression, life, liberty, and so on are put beyond the power of the state to control.

Important for our study of inviolability are Beatty's comments on the second constraint, i.e., the separation of powers. He notes:[11]

> Although there is wide variation among countries in the degree to which the executive and legislative branches are kept separate and apart, in all liberal-democratic states the judicial branch stands alone and is quite independent of the other two.

A modern constitution, then, governs not the people but the government itself. It provides the essential framework for orderly government, its interrelations, its limits. Of signal importance is the role of the judiciary, whose duty it is to uphold the constitution, to be its protector and preserver and guarantor, because the judiciary is the guardian of the constitution and the laws enacted under it.[12]

However, in addition to an independent judiciary, one needs a respect for human and civil rights. After all, the practice of the constitution may not conform to the constitutional text. Examples abound in those countries that were formerly behind the Iron Curtain. Another example is Amendment XV of the Constitution of the United States, enated in 1870, five years following the end of the Civil War, which states:

> The right of citizens of the United States to vote shall not be denied or abridged by the United States or by any state on account of race, color or previous condition of servitude.

Nothing could be clearer, but it took nearly one hundred years to be put into practice because the equality principle was impotent in the context of a community that was apathetic or hostile (Southern states). If this could happen in the United States, where respect for the Constitution and its highest court is strong, it could happen and does happen elsewhere.

With this outlook we tackle the question of the inviolability of a member of the legislative body of government. When and how did this idea arise? Where and how has it spread? Why and how should we end it?

There is no easy answer. But we can chart the past series of events that led to our present situation, choose the goal we wish to reach, and map the route to get there.

The goal is to advance across planet earth the rule of law, equality before the law and good governance. What does this mean?

Many accounts of the "rule of law"* identify its origins in classical Greek thought. Yet for half a millennium, sometimes known as the Dark Ages, Greek thought was almost entirely lost to the West, until rediscovered and given new life in the High Middle Ages by religious scholars. In the 13th century, Albert the Great, a keen student of Arabic learning and culture, adopted for theologians Aristotle's works in philosophy and logic and initiated the Scholastic method (application of Aristotelian methods to Christian doctrines) developed at length by Thomas Aquinas.

In the fifth century B.C. Athens, then at the height of its glory, took great pride in being a democracy governed directly by its citizens, who participated directly in giving rise to the law in its courts and assemblies. Thus democracy was synonymous

---

* For what follows I rely on Prof. Brian Tamanaha's text On The Rule of Law History, Politics, Theory 2004, Cambridge U. Press.

for the Athenians with the rule of law. Law was – literally – the product of the activities of its citizens in the courts and assemblies. The role of these courts and assemblies was to respect the law and to act as guardians of the law, not to declare the law as they pleased. The result was to maintain a democratic system while subordinating the principle of popular sovereignty to the principle of sovereignty of law.

While the Athenian democrats were predominantly worried about capture of the government by aristocratic oligarchies, Plato and Aristotle were concerned about the potential for tyranny in a populist democracy. Law represented an enduring and unchanging order. Plato insisted that the government should be bound by the law. Neither advocated rebellion against the law, even unjust laws. Aristotle held that absolute monarchy or the arbitrary rule of a sovereign is contrary to nature and that the rule of law is preferable to that of an individual. Aristotle's contrast between the rule of law as reason and the "rule of man" as passion has endured through the ages.

The positive Roman contribution to the rule of law was Cicero's insistence that the law must be for the good of the community and comport with natural law. The supremacy of law must be consistent with justice. The negative aspect stems from the commencement of the rule of emperors in 27 BC. Justinian's Code in the sixth century A.D. contained two declarations relevant to the rule of law: "What has pleased the prince has the force of law" and "the prince is not bound by the laws." However a separate provision of the Code asserted: "It is a statement worthy of the majesty of a ruler for the prince to profess himself bound by the laws." In practice, then, the emperors did not quite exercise unfettered legal absolutism. Precedents and practice and professions of being bound by the laws came to impose real, subtle constraints on legal conduct. Lawmakers need to be subject to the law.

The rule of law tradition grew and developed slowly in an unplanned manner in the Middle Ages, owing to three contributing sources: the contest between kings and popes for supremacy, Germanic customary law, and the Magna Carta, which epitomized the effort of nobles to use law to impose restraints on sovereigns.

The arrogation of ultimate power to popes – severely tempered in practice by their limited military strength – was not absurd in the heart of the Middle Ages, when the Holy Roman Empire of the West was united only in being Christian. The Church, it must be appreciated, encompassed everyone in medieval society*, no less emperors and kings, excluding only infidels. Medieval thought in general was saturated in every part with the conceptions of the Christian faith. Hence society was governed by a law identified with Christian justice: the monarch was a Christian, a subject to this law, like everyone else, and made an explicit oath confirming his subjugation to the higher (natural, divine and customary) law and the positive law. From Charlemagne on, monarchs were crowned in a cathedral. The absolutist monarchy inherited from Roman law was thereby counteracted and transformed into a monarchy explicitly under law. The late permeation of Germanic customary law with Christian understandings solidified the identification of law with justice. The key underlying notion was fealty, in which both ruler and ruled were bound to the law; law imposed reciprocal, albeit unequal, obligations that ran in both directions, including loyalty and allegiance. This notion ran through the gamut of social relations of the feudal system.

In medieval understandings the "rule of law" was oriented to containing rapacious kings, and emphasized that law must

---

* Church and society were one, and neither could be changed without the other undergoing a similar transformation. This is the clue to a large part of European history whether secular or ecclesiastical. (R.W. Southern, p. 16)

be for the good of the community. The constitutional struggles of the seventeeth century in England helped to establish the principles of the rule of law. In the nineteenth century, A.V. Dicey, author of <u>Introduction to the Study of the Law of the Constitution</u>, added that everyone is equal before the ordinary law.[13]

In the classical period and the medieval period the supremacy accorded to the rule of law was directly linked to the belief that the content of the law was morally right and was oriented to the good of the community. Whenever implemented, the rule of law should always be subject to evaluations from the standpoint of justice and the good of the community.

It is commonplace wisdom that the defining characteristic of the Western political tradition is "freedom under the rule of law," yet support for the rule of law is not exclusive to the West. Testimonials have come from leaders of a variety of systems, some of which have rejected democracy and individual rights, some of which are avowedly Islamic, some of which reject capitalism, and many of which oppose liberalism and are even explicitly anti-liberalism.[*] The reasons they articulate the rule of law might differ; some do so in the interest of freedom, some in the preservation of order, many in the furtherance of economic development, but all identify it as essential. This apparent unanimity in support of the rule of law is an achievement unparalleled in history. No other singular political ideal has ever achieved global endorsement.

Its frequent repetition is compelling evidence that adherence to the rule of law is an accepted worldwide

---

[*] Robert Mugabe, embattled President of Zimbabwe, previously stated that 'Only a government that subjects itself to the Rule of law has any moral right to demand of its citizens obedience to the Rule of law.' (Tamanaha,p.2)

measure of government legitimacy. But few ever articulate precisely what it means.

Authoritarian governments that claim to abide by the rule of law routinely understand the phrase in oppressive terms. As Chinese law professor Li Shuguang put it, "Chinese leaders want rule *by* law, not rule *of* law [...]. The difference [...] is that under the rule of law, the law is pre-eminent and can serve as a check against the abuse of power. Under rule by law, the rule can serve as a mere tool for a government that suppresses in a legalistic fashion."[14] A terrible example is Germany after the election of 1933.

The rule of law thus stands in the peculiar state of being the pre-eminent shibboleth in the world today without agreement upon precisely what it means.[15] For purposes of our study we fix upon the view of the former chief justice of Ontario, the Honourable Charles Dubin:

> "Constitutionalism" and "rule of law" describe a society in which government officials must act in accordance with the law. For this to be a reality, remedies must be available to citizens when officials act outside the law. This in turn requires an independent judiciary and an independent legal profession. One of the principles upon which a free and democratic society is founded is the supremacy of the rule of law. But the rule of law is not a law in itself, it is dependent upon acquiescence and not force. It is premised on the proposition that once an issue has been resolved after all legal recourse has been resorted to, it will be acquiesced in, leaving it to those who are dissatisfied to seek by legal and democratic means to change the law or the way the law is administered if they think it is unjust.[16]

More than an ideal, however, the rule of law is an achievement, albeit limited to date, in certain parts of what

Barbara Ward calls "spaceship earth" and Marshall McLuhan "the global village."

Our modern liberal-democratic states attest this. For example, this is the present state of affairs in the United Kingdom (U.K.), the United States of America (U.S.A.), Canada, Australia, and most other Commonwealth parliaments. In theory at least, it is so in the member states of the European Union since they are also subject, inter alia, to the 1950 <u>Rome Convention for the Protection of Human Rights and Fundamental Freedoms</u> whose preamble affirms "that they have a common heritage of...the rule of law."

The rule of law, then, is both an ideal and an achievement, partially realized, always to be better achieved, subject to the human reality of progress and decline, always a work in progress in the unfolding Hegelian dialectic of thesis, antithesis, synthesis. It encompasses both substantive justice and process, both judicially unenforceable hortatory declarations of intent (such as contained in the <u>Declaration of Rights of Man and the Citizen</u> of August 26, 1789 in France, where the rule of law is specifically referred in no less than nine of the seventeen articles),[17] and concrete judicially enforceable remedies available equally to those high born or of low estate. It asserts that all persons are under the rule of law, both sovereign and subject, both leaders and led.

Such is the ideal, the partial reality, the global goal. Our next chapter charts past British experience to highlight its characteristic contribution to the European tradition of government. The British idea of law-boundedness and limited monarchy[18] advanced the concrete realization of the rule of law without need to assert the idea of the inviolability of a member of parliament.

Chapter 2
The British Experience

The struggle between Crown and Parliament provides the ongoing context for the British historical experience. Freedom from arrest and freedom of speech are the two key parliamentary privileges that result. These privileges translate into immunity from arrest in certain circumstances and immunity from legal consequences, criminal and civil, for words spoken in Parliament. Freedom of speech is the key freedom. Freedom from arrest, however, also essential, occurs first, both chronologically and practically. It starts in the early period of the English Parliament. It first concerns members' attendance at meetings, an ancient concept from Roman times as the reader will recall from the introductory chapter.

Freedom from Arrest

Whatever its origin, whether in some recollection of the freedom to attend traditional popular assemblies or in the freedom of the King's servants to do their work in Parliament (which in medieval times was primarily a court of justice, the High Court of Parliament), freedom to attend Parliament was clearly established at an early date. Parliament was both the time and the place to petition for favours and to remedy wrongs.[19] The High Court of Parliament consisted of the Crown and the Lords temporal. The Crown's entourage enjoyed the protection of the Crown – the King's peace. Litigation in a lower tribunal was not to impede the King's servants from their work in Parliament.

The King's peace was not for the Lords temporal only. Members of the Commons claimed and eventually won this same Crown protection.

The first known assertion of freedom from arrest by the Commons, separately from the Lords, seems to date from 1340 when the King released a member from prison during the Parliament following that in which he had been prevented by his detention from taking his seat.[20]

In 1404, the English Commons claimed that its members were protected by privilege from arrest for debt, contract or trespass of any kind, according to the custom of the realm. The courts in 1472 accepted that members were protected by custom from being arrested, imprisoned or impeded for debt during the time of Parliament. In 1429, the Commons accepted that privilege could not be pleaded against criminal offences, then adequately summed up as treason, felony and breach of the peace.

This distinction between civil and criminal proceedings is explained by the priority accorded to the public interest. Serious criminal offences concerned the public interest. The criminal law applied to protect the public interest or state security. This trumped the need for a member to attend regular parliamentary proceedings.

Civil proceedings, however, were of a private nature. The fundamental principle of the ancient law and custom of Parliament was clear in this regard. As the House of Lords stated:[21]

> Unless Parliament could keep its membership intact, free from outside interference, whether or not the interference was with the motive of embarrassing its action, it could not be confident of any accomplishment. The privilege reflected the priority accorded to the public interest in the

regular attendance of a Member of Parliament over the private interest in the uninterrupted application of the civil legal process.

This immunity from civil suit, originally founded on the ancient law and custom of Parliament, was intended to prevent actions against members in their absence due to attendance in Parliament. But today, in the United Kingdom and Canada, a member may be sued for what he does or says beyond a proceeding in Parliament. Any attempt to postpone an action for reasons of immunity will fail. Thus, if a member does not attend interlocutory proceedings such as a pre-trial examination for discovery, he or she will suffer the consequences. For example, the member's statement of defence could be struck out or a default judgment entere against the member.

Freedom of Speech

This is the most important parliamentary privilege giving rise to immunity from legal process, civil or criminal. We can trace its origin in England to the parliament of Edward III (1313-1374) and, like freedom from arrest, to the medieval concept of parliament as primarily a court of justice, the High Court of Parliament. The English House of Commons asserted this freedom, separately from the Lords, until by usage and custom it eventually became part of the law of Parliament.

Nevertheless, the claim had a stormy start. When one Haxey, a former King's clerk, offered a bill to Parliament to reduce the excessive charge of the Royal Household, the King was not amused. His displeasure condemned Haxey to death as a traitor. Happily, both the Commons and the House of Lords brought a successful petition to the subsequent King to reverse the condemnation (1396-1397).

Notwithstanding the Haxey episode, the privilege of freedom of speech as against the Crown appears to have been acknowledged from the beginning. In his 1908 book, The Procedure of the House of Commons: A Study of its History and Present Form, Josef Redlich wrote:

> They did oftentimes, say Elsynge, under Edward III, discuss and debate amongst themselves many things concerning the King's prerogative and agreed upon petitions for laws to be made directly against his prerogative, as may appear by divers of the said petitions, yet they were never interrupted in their consultations, nor received, check for the same, as may appear also by the answers to the said petitions.[22]

By the latter part of the fifteenth century the Commons seems to have enjoyed an undefined right of freedom of speech. But this was a matter of tradition rather than a privilege claimed and obtained. It was more a question of "it's always been so" than "that's an essential right for the proper functioning of Parliament."

A shift of emphasis from traditional assumptions to a claim of privilege for the House appears in the petition of Speaker Sir Thomas More in 1523. That petition asks King Henry VIIII "to take all in good part, interpreting every man's words, how uncunningly soever they may be couched, to proceed yet of a good zeal towards the profit of your Realm and honour of your royal person."

The principal function for the speaker at that time was to act as mouthpiece of the Commons and communicate the resolutions of the Commons to the King. The King did not look kindly on those meddling in affairs of state. This prompted Shakespeare's Bolingbroke (who became Henry IV in 1399) to refer to the last of the Plantagenet speakers as "a caterpillar of this Commonwealth which I have sworn to weed and pluck away." (Richard II, Act II, Sc. 3) He did just that and Speaker Bussy was the first to meet a violent end. In the next hundred and some years, eight more followed, not, as is often supposed, in consequence of their activities as speaker but rather because of their involvement in the losing side of royal politics. Two former speakers died by the axe on the same day in 1510.*

We know with certainty, however, that by the first Parliament of Elizabeth in 1558 a claim for freedom of speech in debate was made, that in 1563 it was justified as "according to an ancient order," and that by the end of the century it was a regular practice. Nevertheless, the Queen made it clear on various occasions that she did not intend the privilege to be taken literally. Thus, while the privilege had become an established precedent in the view of Parliament, in reality it was a concession of a very doubtful nature in the ongoing battle between Crown and Parliament.

In 1610 the House of Commons asserted that freedom of speech "could not well be taken from us without shaking the foundations of the liberties of Parliament." In 1621, James I challenged these assumptions. Privileges, he said, "were derived from the grace and permission of our ancestors and us." To this the House rejoined in the famous protestation in 1621 that "every Member of the House of Commons hath freedom from all impeachment, imprisonment and molestation, other than by censure of the House itself, for or concerning any bill, speaking, reasoning or declaring of any matter or matters touching the Parliament business." In 1629, Sir John Elliot and two other members of the House of Commons were arrested and found guilty in the Court of King's Bench for words spoken in the House deemed to be seditious.

---

* See Maingot, Parliamentary Privilege in Canada, 2nd, 1997, pp. 276-277. See also The Office of The Speaker of the Parliaments of the Commonwealth, Philip Laundy, Quiller Press Ltd., London, 1986.

In the short-lived Parliament of 1640, John Pym defended the privileges of the Commons in these memorable words which apply today:*

> The privileges of Parliament were not given for the ornament or advantage of those who are the members of Parliament. We are free from suits that we may the more entirely addict ourselves to the public services; we have liberty of speech that our counsels may not be corrupted with fear, or our judgments perverted with self respects. Those three great faculties and functions of Parliament, the legislative, judiciary, and consiliary power, cannot be well exercised without such privileges as these. The wisdom of our laws, the faithfulness of our counsels, the righteousness of our judgments, can hardly be kept pure and untainted if they proceed from distracted and restrained minds. These powers of Parliament are to the body politic as the rational faculties of the soul to a man: that which keeps all the parts of the Commonwealth in frame and temper ought to be most carefully preserved in that freedom, vigour and activity which belongs to itself.[23]

The struggle for freedom of speech reached its climax during the reign of Charles I, when the long constitutional conflict between the Crown and Parliament came to a head. On January 4, 1641 (1642 according to our present calendar), the King, attended by an armed escort, entered the Commons chamber and attempted to arrest five members on a charge of treason resulting from their proceedings in the House. He took the Speaker's chair and called upon the five members by name, but the House maintained an angry silence. He then turned to the Speaker and demanded that the members be

---

* John Pym (1584-1643) English politician who in 1641 took a leading part in the impeachment of the Earl of Stafford, helped to draw up the Grand Remonstrance, and in 1642 was one of the five members whom Charles I singled out by name.

pointed out to him, upon which the Speaker, Lenthall, fell on his knees and delivered his famous reply: "May it please Your Majesty, I have neither eyes to see, nor tongue to speak in this place, but as the House is pleased to direct me, whose servant I am here..."* The entry in the <u>Journal of the House of Commons</u> for the following day shows clearly and in no uncertain terms the view which the House took of the King's unwarranted intrusion: "That the same is a high breach of the Rights and Privilege of Parliament, and inconsistent with the Liberties and Freedom thereof ..."**

The privilege and immunities of Parliament were never effectively challenged after the restoration of the monarchy in 1660, and freedom of speech was finally confirmed after the Revolution of 1688 by the <u>Bill of Rights</u> which declared in Article 9: "That the freedom of speech, and debates or proceedings in Parliament, ought not to be impeached or questioned in any court or place out of Parliament."***

---

* The distinguishing feature of the U.S. Congress is that the Speaker plays a partisan and quite influential role in the legislative process. The French Bureau Model has a Speaker who is not strictly an impartial official, but who also does not control the legislative agenda or the legislature's administration.

** This incident has been well known and frequently cited for years; but most of the interest aroused by it has been connected with liberty of the subject rather than rights of parliament. There came a time in the nineteenth century when these two concepts had to be separated, because even a representative institution can become autocratic; but for a long period, privilege of parliament was defended as one of the chief means of upholding and preserving the liberty of the subject. (Mary Patterson Clarke, <u>Parliamentary Privilege in the American Colonies</u>, 1943, New Haven, Conn., Yale University Press, p. 1.

*** The House of Commons boldly but mistakenly asserted its authority in 1689 when two judges of the Court of King's Bench were brought before the House, questioned and taken into the custody of the Sergeant at Arms for a decision they rendered against the Sergeant at Arms who had taken a Member into custody pursuant to an order of the House. This was in time the object of severe judicial censure. (See Maingot, pp. 276-277).

John Hatsell, author of <u>Precedents of Proceedings of the House of Commons</u> (U.K., 1818), emphasized the fact that privilege is intended solely to guard the functions of Parliament undisturbed. It is not for the advantage of a member. He examined the privileges of members of the House of Commons from earliest times to the end of the Parliament of 1628 and observed:

> The principal view, which the House of Commons seem always to have had in the several declarations of their privileges, was this 'of securing to themselves, (1) their right of attendance in Parliament, unmolested by threats or insults from private person; (2) their thoughts and attention undisturbed by any concern for their goods or estate; (3) their personal presence in the House, not to be withdrawn, either by the summons of inferior courts; by the arrest of their bodies in civil cause; or, which was of more importance, by commitment by orders from the Crown, for any supposed offences.' Beyond this they seem never to have attempted to go; there is not a single instance of a member's claiming the privilege of Parliament, to withdraw himself from the criminal law of the land: for offences against the public peace they always thought themselves amenable to the laws of their country; they were contented with being substantially secured from any violence from the Crown, or its ministers, but readily submitted themselves to the judicature of the King's Bench, the legal Court of criminal jurisdiction....[24]

Erskine May, author of <u>Erskine May's Treatise on the Law, Privileges, Proceedings and Usage of Parliament</u> (now in its twenty-third edition, 2004), confirms that as early as the middle of the seventeeth century both Houses of Parliament gave expression to the principle that "Privilege of Parliament is granted in regard of a service of the Commonwealth and is not to be used to the danger of the Commonwealth."[25]

Let us now see how Canada, a Commonwealth offshoot of the British experience, has developed.

Canada, like other countries whose parliaments have grown up with the British Westminster model, restricts privilege, and thus immunity, to the function of a member when occupied in a parliamentary proceeding. It thus rejects the concept and practice of parliamentary inviolability. It affirms the basic freedom of a member to participate in open, honest, and free debate, the freedom to speak openly which is essential to every free council, assembly, and legislative body. As the Ontario Court of Appeal put it in 1971,[26] such freedom of speech is essential "to protect him from harassment in and out of the House in his legitimate activities in carrying on the business of the House."

Long before, in 1878, the Supreme Court of Canada affirmed that, "one of the first and greatest of its privileges is free speech and one of the advantages of the legislative bodies is the right of exposing and denouncing abuses by means of free speech."[27]

Not all parliaments enjoy this complete freedom of speech. A review of the immunity provisions of the 85 of 140 parliaments that replied to the Inter-Parliamentary Union Reference Compendium of 1986 shows that some parliaments make their members responsible for statements in parliament which are slanderous, treasonous, or negatively reflect in some manner on the state.[*]

The nature of the privilege of freedom of speech was recently very much at issue in Canada. The question concerned whether the testimony of a witness before a parliamentary committee was privileged. The witness in question had

---

[*] The countries are Albania, Armenia, Bahrain, Belarus, Germany, Greece, Hungary, Latvia, Lithuania, Malaysia, Maldives, Morocco, Mozambique, Ukraine, Yemen, Sierra Leone and the Maldives.

already appeared before a parliamentary committee and was now testifying before the Commission of Inquiry into the sponsorship programs and advertising activities known as the Gomery Commission, the name of the commissioner heading it, Justice John Gomery. One of the parties before the Commission alleged that the witness had made prior statements to the parliamentary committee which were inconsistent with his testimony now before the Commission. That party wanted to introduce into evidence before the Commission the allegedly inconsistent prior statements. Parliamentary privilege (immunity) was claimed concerning the prior statements. The House of Commons rejected the request of the Commission to consider waiving parliamentary privilege. The Commissioner said the privilege belongs to the House and not to the member and agreed that the Commission should not be seen to encroach in any way upon the privilege and immunities of the Parliament of Canada. Accordingly, he ruled on November 22, 2004 that the prior statements could not be introduced into evidence and that the witness could not be asked questions based on them.

One may indeed go further. In light of its historical development and our growing understanding, one may say the privilege belongs to the people whose English representatives embodied it in a resolution of the House and enacted the privilege in a law, the statute called the Bill of Rights, in 1689. That law is also the law of Canada. To amend or repeal it requires an Act of Parliament, not simply a resolution of one of the Houses of Parliament. Freedom of speech, it may confidently be asserted today, intends not so much the protection of a member against civil or criminal proceedings. It intends the protection of the liberty of the people by freeing their elected members to represent them in Parliament, without fear of such legal proceedings.[28]

An English Parliamentarian Was Not Your Average Citizen: Privilege of Peerage

Before moving to the experience of continental Europe, let us complete this chapter with an historical overview of a significant reality: an English member of Parliament was not your average citizen, and a member of the House of Lords had, in addition to parliamentary privilege or immunity, the privilege of peerage. This provides some insight into why there was no need to develop parliamentary inviolability (protection from the criminal process beyond the precincts of Parliament) as part of the immunities of English parliamentary law.

A good starting point is the document known as Magna Carta. Although subsequent interpretive adumbrations seek to convince us it was the basis of English constitutional liberties, it was in fact a political document produced in a crisis. The beleaguered King John, in return for pledges of continued loyalty from his barons, undertook not to further encroach on their traditional prerogatives and jurisdiction.* It was devised mainly in the interests of the aristocracy, and the "free man" it referred to was a class forming a small portion of the population of thirteenth century England.[29] It has been called the most famous restraint upon royal authority.[30] Briefly, it came about in the following way.

King John provoked his barons to rebellion with his military failures in France, his stringent taxation, and his abuse of royal and feudal privileges. Although some grievances were personal, the barons wanted mainly to protect themselves from encroachment of royal authority. In 1215 they drew up a charter and sent it to King John for his approval under the royal seal. He refused. The barons then renounced allegiance

---

* Appearing for the Crown, A Legal and Historical Review of Criminal Prosecutorial Authority in Canada, Philip C. Stenning, A Study Conducted for the Law Reform Commission of Canada, 1986, p. 7.

to him, marched on London, and captured it. King John realized that he had to settle with them and agreed to meet them at Runnymede. There, on June 15, 1215, he confirmed the charter with his seal and issued it.

Magna Carta contained the first detailed definition of the relationship between King and barons, guaranteed feudal rights, abolished many abuses of feudal tenures, and much more. It brought regularity to the judicial system, set the Court of Common Pleas permanently at Westminster, simplified the conduct of trials with strict procedural rules, and brought in standard penalties for felonies. Condemnation on rumour and suspicion was ended. Evidence based on credible witnesses was now required.

But it was a product of the feudal age expressing feudal law and custom. At the time it was issued, it did not hold the constitutional significance it acquired later on. For example, its famous Article 39, which said that "no free man shall be taken or imprisoned or disseised or outlawed or exiled or in any way ruined, nor will we go and send against him except by lawful judgment by his peers and by the law of the land," concerned only the barons, not the population at large. The aristocrats and others, but not the serf, were the free men intended by the expression "free man".*

Here we note that privilege of peerage and privilege of parliament are not identical. The elusive distinction may better be grasped by looking at the origin of privilege of peerage. It derived from the fact that, as major tenants-in-chief of the Sovereign, the peers (Lords) were full members of his court; they therefore could not, in ancient times, be proceeded against in the courts below, which regarded their persons

---

* Indeed, as Anne Pallister has pointed out, a 17th century writer asked how he could revere a charter which upholds the privileges of the oppressors of the people. See her Magna Carta, 1971, Clarendon Press, p. 18.

as "for ever sacred and inviolable." Thus it came to pass by a mixture of heredity and royal favour that members of the House of Lords enjoyed the form of inviolability known as privilege of peerage: the right to be tried by their peers for the crimes of treason and felony.

Attempts to catch the elusive nature of the parliamentary peerage, from which parliamentary inviolability sprang, in the butterfly net of reason have almost always failed.[31] Even more, the butterfly flits from flower to flower with an insouciance that baffles the butterfly catcher.

The first mention of the judgment of peers occurs in Article 39 of Magna Carta of King John. It was always considered the statutory basis of the right of peers to be tried by peers. While it went beyond the barons, the Great Charter expressed the reality that the King needed his court and counsel and the court and counsel needed the King. A quid pro quo existed; part of it included that members of his council, the barons, would be judged by the barons, in their courts, especially where, on the prosecution of the King, there was peril of life and member, or peril of disinheritance.

King John bound himself in such a manner as to show that "judgment of peers" was one thing, the "law of the land" another. The "judgment of peers" was a very simple matter and well understood at the time. The "law of the land" included all legal proceedings, criminal or civil, other than the judgment of peers. The judgment of peers had reference chiefly to the right of landholders to their lands, or to some matters connected with feudal tenures and its incidents.

In spite of a long struggle for their own courts of law, the barons only succeeded in establishing that Lords should be tried by Lords for crimes of treason and felony. Thus tenants holding with obligations and loyalty under a Lord or baron, had cases heard in the barons court composed of other tenants of that Lord. Lords, holding equally with obligation and loyalty under the King, had their cases heard by fellow Lords.

From the time of the Conquest, the spiritual Lords had attempted to escape lay jurisdiction. From 1553 onwards, it seems to have been settled law that bishops do not enjoy the right of being tried by peers.* Also, in trials of peers on indictment of treason or felony the judgment was always that of the temporal Lords alone. With regard to less serious crimes, i.e., those other than treason and felony, it was established by law in 1548 that a peer might commit housebreaking, highway robbery, horse stealing and robbing of churches, once, without punishment.[32] As early as 1154 during the reign of Henry II there existed in the Exchequer Court the privilege that a baron gave his word instead of taking the oath. Until the year 1751, when a Lord was a party in a civil action, there had to be knights upon the jury. For a time, the necessity of proceeding by "original writ" against a peer had, while it existed, the effect of making actions against peers more expensive, and consequently more difficult.[33] Until 1875, a Bill in Chancery was a mode of commencing an action, and while an answer thereto had to be made on oath by a commoner, a peer need only make answer on his honour.[34]

Parliament confirmed Magna Carta in 1216-1217 during the reign of Henry III, King John's son. Under Edward I, in 1297 Parliament again confirmed it in a modified form, now the standard one. During the early seventeenth century, Magna Carta became the battle cry of opponents of the royal prerogative during the parliamentary rebellion. The 1628 Petition of Right and the 1689 Bill of Rights buttressed Magna Carta. All this provided the solid foundation for the assertion of parliamentary supremacy over the Crown and provided a

---

* Pike, A Constitutional History of the House of Lords, from original sources, p. 226.

documentary basis for the rule of law in England. Major credit for the creative extension of Magna Carta, from the status of a compact between King and barons to the constitutional foundation for the liberties of all English freemen, goes to the great English jurist, Sir Edward Coke, and the parliamentarians who heeded his interpretation.

But class privilege did not disappear, and its reality helps explain why in England there developed a very real practical difference between the privileged class and the others as regards the "criminal law." It helps explain why members of Parliament, and particularly members of the House of Lords enjoying privilege of peers, had little concern for protection from criminal law beyond the precincts of parliament or from the Crown or "la puissance des baïonnettes" (see Chapter 4). They were already protected by the rule of law that was congealing into existence, the common law, the courts, and a stratified society that in fact distinguished between the privileged few and the many others, the "crimes" of the elite and the "crimes" of the others.

An important element of the pre-Conquest English government, one that King William carried on with little change in the years immediately following the Conquest, was the "witenagemot", the embryonic House of Lords, the national assembly of the "witan", the "wise men" of the land. The word "witenagemot" only came into use toward the end of the first millennium, and it was not before the eleventh century that it became the official term to describe formal assemblies of the King's counsellors; even then it was not of very frequent occurrence, so far as evidence of contemporary or non-contemporary chronicles goes. The chronicles give little evidence as to the composition of the witenagemot. Usually it is stated simply that a witenagemot or council was held for such and such a purpose. More precise information as to what sort of person would be present is afforded by the list of witnesses generally appended to charters issued at times when the witenagemot was meeting, to record grants of land and privileges by the King.[35]

The longest list of witnesses is appended to the charter of 1044. It is headed, as invariably in charters of the period, by the King's own name. After the royal family come the churchmen, the archbishops of Canterbury and York followed by bishops and abbots.

The witness list of two charters issued in 1068 give a good idea of the kinds of people who would be present on such an occasion immediately after the Conquest. They show how strong the continuity from the witenagemot of the Conqueror's predecessors was. At the head of the lists of witnesses to both charters appear the King and Queen, then the King's son. After the royal family come the clergy, the archbishops of Canterbury and York and the bishops and abbots. Then come the courts (dukes) of Normandy and the English earl, greater and lesser landowners, clerics and officers.

This high position of churchmen in royal councils was common to all parts of Western Europe in the Middle Ages. Partly it was due to the recognition of their sacred station; and partly it reflected the practical necessity of obtaining the counsel of the only fully educated class of society (i.e. even the upper classes of the laity were unable to read or write Latin). From the early days of Christianity, churchmen and Church Latin dominated the councils of English kings. On various occasions the bishops and the King together, without lay witan, made up the whole assembly.

From the beginning of the Norman kings, the proclamations declare that the King is crowned by the common consent of the barons. Thus while they were the King's tenants in common, their counsel was necessary for the amendment of laws and for decisions affecting their land. While their courts heard litigants from among their freemen and vassals, their own complaints were dealt with in the council of the king.

To try to write a comprehensive history of the Lords, including their claim to being "forever sacred and inviolable", would be like trying to write a comprehensive history of Asia: to describe one landmark is to ignore a hundred others, to single out a village for attention to miss cities of far greater importance. Very little has been written in defence of the hereditary principle, and that which has been written has generally been composed under the threat of its abolition. Yet that principle is recognized at work throughout European civilization as it existed before 1789.[36] To compare France and England before that moment, France was an absolute monarchy, England was a mixed monarchy, a dominum politicum et regale, the power shared between, first, the Lords and the King, and then between Parliament and the King. Erasmus has described it as a limited monarchy kept in check by aristocracy and democracy.

It will be seen in Chapter 3 that the parliamentary inviolability that was established in the National Assembly of France on June 23, 1789, was born to protect its members against "la puissance des baïonnettes," the power of the bayonets. This was not the case for the English House of Lords whose form of parliamentary immunity resulted from their status as the King's counsellors and members of his court. In the English bicameral Parliament, the House of Commons members enjoyed the same rights as non-members outside their precincts when it came to the law. They were tried before the courts of the land, not by their peers.

The early English system of criminal law had almost no formal machinery for the prosecution of criminal cases. It was not under the exclusive control of public authorities. It relied heavily on the initiative of private individuals. The role of private prosecution in the administration of the criminal law was crucial. Until the state assumed the management of crime in the nineteenth century and professional police forces took over the pursuit and apprehension of suspects, the gathering of evidence, the preparation of cases, and the burden of prosecution – and indeed decisions about which cases would be taken to trial and which would not – were matters left largely to the private initiative and discretion of the victim. The role of the state (i.e., the Crown) was confined substantially to direct interventions in matters in which the Sovereign had a particular interest.

The Crown intervened usually in either of two ways. In some cases, especially those with political overtones, the Sovereign initiated and conducted prosecutions through his or her personal representative. In other cases, those initiated by private individuals, the Sovereign through a personal representative intervened to terminate them prior to their conclusions. [37]

Political life was the proper sphere of the landed interest alone.* The political elite controlled Parliament. There was a close relationship between law, property and power.

When members of the elite were indicted for crimes widely recognized as such, like rape, robbery, or theft, they were usually acquitted. Political influence, family patronage, jury deference to their oligarchic rulers, the skill of expensive counsel, all played their part. Behaviour that would not have been tolerated in the "lower orders" was deemed merely "letting off steam" on the part of gentlemen.[38]

---

* English Social History, <u>A Survey of Six Centuries, Chaucer to Queen Victoria, G.M. Trevelyan, 1942, Longmans, Green & Co</u>, London, N.Y., Toronto, p. 295.

Most Englishmen, even into the eighteenth century, were illiterate and parliamentary representation was rooted in the class system. A distinction then imposed itself between the literate and illiterate, between what today we call crime in the boardrooms and crime in the streets, then called acts in the suites and acts in the streets. Thus one critic has written: "Crime in the eighteenth century was after all an act on the streets rather than the suites. Generally speaking, men like the Duke of Newcastle (Prime Minister, 1757-1762) or Sir Robert Walpole (Prime Minister 1721-1742) succeeded in abstaining from street robbery or the theft of wood, and they thus escape our attention in the criminal records."[39]

In sum, the law was twisted for the benefit of the rich and powerful. The elite lived in a different world*. As we ascend the social scale, the very concept of crime becomes problematical. The elite activity of duelling offers a striking example.

Duelling was officially a crime, which Blackstone described as "murder with malice aforethought." This defined what the law said. The reality was otherwise. The mania for duelling infected polite society, and jurymen overwhelmingly accepted the plea that duelling was a proper way for "gentlemen" to resolve their disputes. Duelling was an instance where the elite

---

* In a word, English law has always been concerned more with credibility and authority than punishment of each and every infraction. That this political culture meshed beautifully with the requirements of the elite has been ably demonstrated by the most convincing explanation yet provided of the 'meaning' of the Bloody Code. As Douglas Hay explains it, in eighteenth century England, the elite used a system of draconian punishments to allay its own anxieties over a number of issues: the real stability of their regime, the threat from Jacobites and later from Jacobins, the fear of the mob. The real motive was credibility. The sanguinary statutes were not meant to be implemented at all times and at all points. As Hay expresss it, they were more concerned with authority than property. The principal aim was always to compel the deference of the lower orders. It was deference – an obvious aspect of the aristocratic tradition – that the authorities wanted, not one hundred per cent effectiveness in punishment or control of crime. (McLynn p.xvi).

clearly committed acts declared criminal by their own code. Three eighteenth-century prime ministers fought duels.[*]

Other examples abound. Well-born people guilty of shoplifting and pickpocketing, crimes that could consign the poverty-stricken to the gallows, were invariably bailed or acquitted. In a rape case the judge directed the jury that they could not find Lord Baltimore guilty when it was simply Sarah Woodcock's word against that of an aristocrat. The jury returned a verdict of "not guilty." William, fifth Lord Byron, killed William Chaworth in an improvised duel in January 1765 in the back room of a Pall Mall tavern. The House of Lords convicted him of manslaughter (not, as Blackstone had clearly stated, murder with malice aforethought), and he was then saved from punishment by the privileges of his rank. The elite thus gave implicit sanction to a practice explicitly condemned by criminal law. This arrogant attitude toward the law taken by the sons and daughters of the elite demonstrated that they had no doubt they were above it. The South Sea Bubble entrenched the popular idea that the only difference between ordinary criminals and elite politicians was the class position they occupied.[**]

The foregoing examples help give context to the English parliamentary experience and development that found no need to claim parliamentary inviolability (special immunity from the criminal process).

The only way elite crime could be dealt with, other than unsatisfactorily through the courts, was by impeachment before Parliament. Usually this procedure was employed in purely political trials. A member of the House of Lords was

---

[*] Prime Minister Fox with Adam, Prime Minister Shelburne with Fullerton, Prime Minister Pitt with Tierney. McLynn, p. 142.

[**] See generally Crime and Punishment in Eighteenth Century England, Chapter 8, Frank McLynn 1989, Routledge, London & N.Y. See also Trevelyan, p 315-316

entitled to be tried by his peers in the case of the crimes of treason and felony. This ancient right was held for seven hundred years and stemmed from the principle that the person of a peer was inviolable and was to be judged by his peers. It was finally surrendered by the peers themselves, who were responsible for inserting the words "privilege of peerage in relation to criminal proceedings is hereby abolished" in the Criminal Justice Act of 1948. Lord de Clifford was the last to be tried, for manslaughter, by his peers in 1935.

The House of Commons used impeachment proceedings to impeach before the House of Lords any peer or commoner for treason or any other crime or misdemeanor beyond the reach of the law, or which no other authority in the state would prosecute. In impeachments, the Commons, as a great representative inquest of the nation, first found the crime, and then, as prosecutor, supported their charge before the Lords. The earliest recorded impeachment was in 1376 and the last was in 1806. There have not been seventy during the whole course of English history. Impeachment in the seventeenth and eighteenth centuries was a means of "liquidating" opponents. It was a means by which Parliament could get rid of unpopular ministers. The acceptance of the principle of cabinet ministers as responsible to Parliament (rather than to the Sovereign) in the early nineteenth century made impeachment unnecessary. The ballot boxes are now available for political opponents and the criminal courts for criminals.

The eighteenth century in the U.K. was a period when the House of Commons not only used impeachment as a "liquidating" measure, but also abused its authority within the parliamentary precincts to commit for contempt by punishing for alleged contempts and factual situations completely unrelated to a proceeding in Parliament. The House stretched the privilege to include the enjoyment of game and the right to try trespassers. The case most frequently cited occurred in 1759 was:

> ... an action of trespass for breaking and entering a fishery tried in the House of Commons, to the lasting opprobrium of parliamentary privilege, to the scandal and disgrace of the House of Parliament that tried it, and to the astonishment and alarm of all good men, whether lawyers or laymen. Admiral Griffin made complaint to the House whereof he was a Member, that three men had broken into and entered his fishery near Plymouth, had taken the fish therefrom, and destroyed the nets therein; and the House forthwith, instead of indignantly and in mockery of such a pretension dismissing the charge and censuring him who made it, ordered the defendants in the trespass, for they must be called, to be committed into the custody of the Sergeant-at-Arms. They were committed into that custody accordingly; they were brought to the Bar of the House of Commons, and there, on their knees, they confessed their fault; they promised never again to offend the admiral by interfering with his alleged right of fishery; and upon this confession and promise they were discharged on paying their fees.[*]

While not in the same league as abuse, the Speaker of the Canadian House of Commons was "permitted" to rule on March 16, 1993 (Debates, <u>House of Commons</u>, p. 17071-2) that a committee of the House dealing with the matter of Unemployment Insurance (U.I.) on March 10, 1993, was correct to expunge all of the evidence of a witness from the International Association of Machinists and Aerospace Workers with which the (government) majority of the committee took offence as being "inflammatory," amongst other things. The

---

[*] Wellesley v. Duke of Beaufort (Mr. Long Wellesley's case) (1831), 2 Russ. & M. 639 at 659-60, and footnote (a), p. 660, where it is pointed out that the Journals of the House of Commons (U.K.) at that period abound with cases of a similar kind. For specific instances, see Stockdale v. Hansard (1839), 9 Ad. & El. 1 at 13, 48 Rev. Rep. 326 at 334.

witness had said, regarding the issue of fraudulent claims for unemployment insurance, that "the proportion of [U.I.] recipients cheating the system is less than the proportion of Tory MPs convicted of corruption".

The Speaker's ruling provoked a public or at least journalistic outcry. The Globe and Mail reported, "the Speaker of the House of Commons upheld the committee's exercise in Stalinist historiography".* While the committee had the power to print its proceedings, what should properly be characterized as a matter of freedom of speech in Parliament was being curtailed, if not assailed.

Notably, immediately after the Speaker made his ruling on March 16, a member of the House rose to point out that the same committee on March 15 had allowed the same evidence to be read into the record by a subsequent witness quoting from a newspaper report, with nary a murmur (It seems that the majority of the committee may have been nudged by their senior House colleagues). The witness said, "Then we have a situation where this committee expels a group for saying that there were more convicted frauds in the Tory caucus than there were among U.I. recipients. I'm quoting The [Montreal] Gazette, which says that 2% of members of the Tory caucus were accused of cheating compared with 0.01% of U.I. claimants."**

It was only shortly after World War II that privilege of peerage in criminal proceedings was abolished in the U.K. In moving the amendment to the Criminal Justice Act that abolished such privilege, the Lord Chancellor on June 7, 1948, told the House of Lords that "we shall in future be treated like everybody else, and if the method is good enough for the

---

* Editorial, March 30, 1993

** Minutes of Proceedings of the Legislative Committee on Bill C-113, March 15, 1993, p. 7). See also Globe and Mail, Toronto. March 29, March 30, 1993; La Presse, Montreal, 30 March, 1993; Toronto Star, March 11, 1993.

other people it is good enough for us… Let us end what is a complete anachronism".

Why, then, did members of parliament on the European continent deem it necessary to claim parliamentary inviolability and continue to make such claim? To that question and the European experience we now turn.

Chapter 3
The Continental European
Experience and Beyond

Complexity marks all history and especially the Middle Ages. Some may therefore find misleading and tendentious such generalizations as those articulated in the following passages:

> ... the church was not a state, it was the state. The state or rather the civil authority (for a separate society was not recognized) was merely the police department of the church.[40]

> ... ecclesiastical influences abounded in the law in England and the continent until the Reformation. Dogmas of theology reigned over all the arts and sciences. None save God could make laws in the Middle Ages.[41]

Yes, monarchs were consecrated in cathedrals and what we call today "Church and State" were intertwined. The complexity of the Middle Ages, however, was far more subtle, as we shall see, arising from the irruption into human history of that unique Jesus of Nazareth who said with understated pithiness, "Render to Caesar the things that are Caesar's and to God the things that are God's" (Luke 20:25). Still today there exists that ongoing problem of unravelling what Jesus intended. What are the things of God and what those of Caesar? Concretely, in the unfolding of human history, this gives rise to the difficult task of each age and place, determining the complex practical implications of the distinction between the spiritual and the temporal authority. Slogans do not suffice. Nor do the assumptions of radical modern secularism.

So it was in the Middle Ages in Western society. From the time that Constantine decided to move his imperial capital from Rome to Constantinople, the West developed quite differently from the East. Imperial authority disintegrated in the West. The power of the emperor was challenged by great church leaders. With the barbarian invasions and the total breakdown of Roman imperial authority in the West, the papacy assumed a new role. Brian Tierney, author of The Crisis of Church and State: 1050-1300, University of Toronto Press, 1988, put this well at page 16:

> In the centuries after Gelasius the role of the papacy in temporal affairs was profoundly modified by the total breakdown of Roman imperial authority in the West. England fell to the Angles and Saxons, Gaul to the Franks, Spain to the Visigoths. In Italy itself a brief period of imperial reconquest – directed from Constantinople by the emperor Justinian (527-65) – was ended in 568 by the invasions of the Lombards, the last of the Teutonic people to ravage Italy ... This situation produced two results of the greatest importance for the future development of church-state relations. First, the popes emerged as temporal governors of Rome and the surrounding region. Then they abandoned their old allegiance to the Byzantine emperors and formed a new alliance with the Frankish Kings that led eventually to a new empire in the West under papal auspices.

What we today usually refer to as "Church and State" did not exist in the West during the Middle Ages. Instead, there existed a merged religious and political community known as Christendom in which the papacy spoke with an authority challenged only by the Emperor. As R.W. Southern, author of <u>Western Society and the Church in the Middle Ages</u>, has explained:

> It seems very likely that the papal coronation of Charlemagne as emperor was intended to show that the pope could delegate imperial authority in the West to whom he would, in accordance with the terms of Constantine's gift. But it is certain that Charlemagne did not acquiesce in his view of his position.[*]

The papal claim to supreme temporal lordship in the West met stiff opposition from the outset. Southern summarizes:

> Indeed it is evident that the idea of a western empire as a means of extending papal authority was a mistake from beginning to end. It was a mistake primarily because in creating an emperor the pope created not a deputy, but a rival or even a master. The theoretical supremacy implied in the act of creation could never be translated into practical obedience to orders given and received.[42]

Nonetheless, papal pretensions grew. Southern provides a fascinating study of this growth during the years c. 1050 to c. 1300, when a new generation of papal lawyers strove mightily and with amazing results to assert a claim of "nothing less than a total papal sovereignty in all the affairs of the Christian community."[43] Our concern is not to trace the growth of papal influence, but simply to point out its existence, its complexity, its inevitability at the time, its unforeseen consequences, its legal achievement. As Southern writes:

> The two main characteristics of medieval government, whether secular or ecclesiastical, were these: the ruler was a dispenser of benefits and a

---

[*] R.W. Southern, <u>Western Society and the Church in the Middle Ages</u>, Pelican Books The Pelican History of the Church, 1990, vol. 2, p. 99. Professor Southern was the Chichele Professor of Modern History at Oxford.

dispenser of justice. He was a dispenser of benefits in the first place because it was the chief way in which a ruler could attract loyalty; generosity was what men expected of the great, and they responded to it. This was the great rule of government from the earliest days... To be able to give was the first law of political life, and there was a close connection between this and the most important function of medieval government, the dispensing of justice.[44]

These two functions went on hand in hand, as Southern explains:

The real reason why government sought jurisdiction was because it was the only practical way in which they could enforce their claims to lordship. But once the process had started, the officials who were created by the process had a strong interest in keeping it going ...

Benefits, then, and justice went hand in hand, and in both these fields the pope outstripped all other rulers. The benefits he could grant were solid and lasting, and the justice he could give was stronger and better than any other.[45]

And so, if we try to enter with sympathetic understanding into the concrete complexity of the Middle Ages, we can reasonably accept Southern's assessment that "the responsibility ... for filling the many gaps and meeting the problems presented by a rapidly developing society lay in the first place with the pope," and that "without the papal supremacy it is inconceivable that any such comprehensive system of law could have ever been developed."[46] I will sum up in Southern's words:

This was the golden age of government, and especially of papal government, before the system had been choked with the vexations of politics and the complications of over-elaboration. Much that was done had no practical effect. Much that was effected would in any case have happened. Yet, when every allowance has been made, we may still say that the papal machinery of government was as effective as any government could be before the late nineteenth century. The papal curia of the thirteenth century was, by any standards that were applicable before the days of modern mechanical aids and salaried officials, a large and efficient organization. Like any other government it was constantly engaged in war or the preparation of war, in diplomacy, in the management of estates, in the assessment and collection of taxes; but by far the most highly developed part of the organization was that which dealt with the various stages of legal processes. There was a complicated organization for hearing petitions and complaints, for recording decisions, for drafting the documents necessary for carrying them out, and for keeping copies of the letters sent out. The office routine for performing these duties in a systematic way was the subject of a specialized literature. At most times there were probably well over a hundred experts at the papal court engaged in legal work. Every important ecclesiastical and secular person or corporation in Europe had to be familiar with the procedure of the papal curia, and the most important had proctors permanently retained to look after their interests in the labyrinth of papal government.[47]

Why this digression into papal authority? Hopefully it gives background and balance to a complicated part of human history where even-handed treatment is often lacking and caricature of papal claims often abounds. Both in England and in France papal claims were asserted. But such claims did not come into play on the question of parliamentary inviolability and it is inaccurate to assert "none save God could make laws in the Middle Ages." Yet English parliamentary law never claimed inviolability for its members while France on the continent did.

Why, then, did a claim to parliamentary inviolability arise on the continent?

With the exception of France, before the advent of royal power, our sources about the political systems of most countries are few and unreliable.

With the arrival of royal power, we know that the demand for liberties on the continent asserted itself with varied aims. As we have seen, in England this demand aimed at the control and subjugation of the administrative functions of the Crown. On the continent, in Lombardy in 1183, it aimed at municipal independence; in the German concessions of 1220 and 1221 and the French charters in 1315, it aimed at aristocratic immunity.[48] But all were agreed on the responsibility of the king, even if only considered a feudal lord, to dispense justice among his vassals. This was accepted because the Crown's tenants-in-chief (who could oppose the vassals most effectively) depended on such responsibility to claim their right to maintain and effectively exploit their own estates. The great men and the king derived their power from the same sources. Nothing was so engrained in their minds as title to property.[49]

But there did not develop on the continent a parliamentary system comparable to England's. Instead there developed in the majority of European kingdoms and principalities in the course of the later Middle Ages a system of the assembly of "estates". Here begins the semblance of organized political representation of the subjects of kings or princes which led, with varying degrees of continuity or discontinuity, to the modern parliaments.

By 1715 monarchy had bifurcated into two forms, unlimited and limited, which in European parlance are called absolute and parliamentary monarchy. Nearly all were unlimited, with France as the archetype. The limited or the parliamentary category included Poland, Sweden for a time, and a small number of the German states; England was the archetype.*

These assemblies of "estates" were the "estates general". They consisted of representatives of the three "estates" or orders of the realm: the higher clergy and the nobility were the two privileged minorities, and the third estate represented the other privileged class, namely, the bourgeois of the town. This representation was based on the traditional social classes. Eventually the three estates together came to speak not only for those social classes but for the whole country. But the voices of the non-privileged peasants and some towns were seldom heard.

The estates general in France and elsewhere were never highly esteemed and were never a real threat to the sovereign or the higher estates. But in France the National Assembly was such a threat. The last meeting of France's Estates General was in 1789, when the deputies of the third estate feared they would be overruled by the two privileged orders in any attempt at reform. This fear led to the formation of the revolutionary National Assembly on June 17, 1789. This in turn signalled the end of representations based on traditional social classes.[50] It also signalled the beginning in France of the claim to parliamentary inviolability.

---

* In France by the end of the fifteenth century, the Estates General could be said to have acquired its main characteristics but it was not nor would ever become an institution. Because the Kings had already levied a permanent direct tax throughout France (the taille), they were able to get along without the Estates General in normal time after 1500 and met thereafter only in times of crisis. In the Teutonic states of the continent, it was the necessity of obtaining for the ruler express grants of taxes to supplement their revenue derived from the incidents of feudal tenure which caused the Estates to be summoned and won for them the position they obtained. The ideas of the divine right of Kings that developed, especially in the 17th century, were found to be incompatible with ideas of representation by the estates. Yet the estates in Mecklenburg outlasted those of any other country, surviving until 1918.

Six days later, on June 23, 1789, speaking in that National Assembly, Honoré Mirabeau affirmed that the person of each deputy was inviolable. This was the reason, he said, for the birth of that revolutionary Assembly, "[n]ée de la nécessité de protéger les membres de la jeune et frêle assemblée constituante des conseils violents qui assiègent le trône."[51]

Patrick Fraisseix gives us Mirabeau's memorable words inviting the members of the Assembly to protect themselves against the power of the bayonets:

> Mirabeau invitant le Tiers-état réuni en assemblée nationale à assurer sa protection contre « la puissance des baïonnettes. Je bénis la liberté de ce qu'elle munit de si beaux fruits dans l'assemblée nationale. Assurons notre ouvrage, en déclarent inviolable la personne des députés aux États Généraux. » [52]

Thus we may venture this affirmation: parliamentary inviolability arises with the French Revolution and spreads throughout the world. The complex reasons for that Revolution are the subject of many studies.[53] But the key to the different developments of national representative institutions in England and France lies in the explanation offered by E.B. Fryde in Historial Studies of the English Parliament: Origins to 1399:

> The explanation of the greater effectiveness and ultimate survival of the English Parliament as against the fading out of the continental estates is to be found in the policy of the monarchy. Everything turned on the question whether a national representative assembly was or was not of use to the King.

In England, between the times of Edward I and Edward III, there were 100 Parliaments called between 1275 and 1376. In comparison, after 1500 in France the Kings got along in normal times without the Estates General.

The estates general were prominent where there was an advanced central government, as in France and Aragon, and their role was more limited where city states were the normal political form, as in Italy. Gradually they won political power at the Crown's expense in the fifteenth and sixteenth centuries, when their powers in many European countries were greater than the Parliament in England. With a subsequent rise in absolutism, however, conflict arose between the assemblies and the Crown. This usually ended in victory for the ruler, so that in the seventeenth and eighteenth centuries the estates general were generally convened only to give formal assent to taxes and to listen passively to the government's decisions (with notable exceptions in Wittenberg and Poland).

On the other hand, in England during the fourteenth century the simultaneous gatherings of barons and prelates for the purpose of forming a high court of justice (parliamentum) and, a representative of knights and burgesses, as deputies of the commonalty, for the consideration of grants of taxes, coalesced: the single assembly that resulted was Parliament in its permanent form.[*] After a transitional stage, in which the clergy, the greater and smaller barons, and the cities and boroughs, seemed likely to adopt the system used in Aragon and Scotland, and another in which the county and borough communities continued to assert an essential difference, the three estates of clergy, lords, and commons, finally emerge as

---

[*] Josef Redlich, vol 1, p. 7.

the political constituents of the nation, or, in their parliamentary form, as the lords spiritual and temporal and the commons.[*]

Members of the estates general did not need protection from the various crowns in Europe for what they said or did, whether during the sittings or beyond. This seems not to have been an issue owing to their privileged social positions.

La puissance des baïonnettes and the notorious « lettres de cachet »[**] may have justified, at that time, the revolutionary

---

[*] 'This familiar formula in either shape bears the impress of history. The term 'commons' is not in itself an appropriate expression for the third estate; it does not signify primarily the simple freemen, the plebs, but the plebs organized and combined in corporate communities, in a particular way for particular purposes.
The commons are the 'communitates' or 'universitates,' the organized bodies of freemen of the shires and towns; and the estate of the commons is the 'communitas communitatum,' the general body into which for the purposes of parliament those communities are combined. The term then, as descriptive of the class of men which is neither noble nor clerical, is drawn from the political vocabulary, and does not represent any primary distinction of class.' Constitutional History of England, Stubbs, vol. II. Clarendon Press Series, 1896, p. 174-5.

[**] In French history, **lettres de cachet** were letters signed by the king of France, countersigned by one of his ministers, and closed with the royal seal, or *cachet*. They contained orders directly from the king, often to enforce arbitrary actions and judgements that could not be appealed. In the case of organized bodies lettres de cachet were issued for the purpose of preventing assembly or to accomplish some other definite act. The provincial estates were convoked in this manner, and it was by a lettres de cachet (in this case, a *lettre de jussipri*), or by showing in person in a *lit de justice*, that the king ordered a parlement (a court of justice) to register a law in the teeth of its own refusal to pass it. The best-known lettres de cachet, however, were penal, by which a subject was sentenced without trial and without an opportunity of defense to imprisonment in a state prison or an ordinary jail, confinement in a convent or a hospital, transportation to the colonies, or expulsion to another part of the realm. The wealthy sometimes bought such letters to dispose of unwanted individuals. In this respect, the lettres de cachet were a prominent symbol of the abuses of the *ancient régime* monarchy, and as such were suppressed during the French Revolution. The Comte de Mirabeau wrote a scathing indictment of lettres de cachet while imprisoned in the dungeon of Vincennes (by lettres de cachet obtained by his father). The treatise was published after his liberation in 1782.

National Assembly and Mirabeau's claim that the person of each deputy was inviolable. But today this claim is challenged, both in France and elsewhere. Hervé Issar, writing in the <u>Revue française de droit constitutionnel</u> in 1994, explained:

> Le principe de l'immunité parlementaire a, depuis 1789, traversé l'histoire constitutionnelle française avec une telle constance que l'on serait naturellement enclin à penser que cette institution présente une réelle utilité pratique ainsi qu'une indéniable légitimité théorique et politique.
>
> Pourtant, l'immunité dont bénéficie le parlementaire français a toujours fait l'objet de sérieuses controverses doctrinales, ainsi que d'une certaine incompréhension de la part du citoyen qui n'a jamais vraiment compris pourquoi, une fois élu, le parlementaire bénéficierait d'une protection particulière d'autant plus choquante que, paradoxalement, elle semble instituer une exception au « principe sacré » de l'égalité devant la loi au profit de ceux qui sont justement en charge de l'affaire.[*]

Chapter 5 addresses this issue in compendious fashion to allow the reader to form a reasoned view. As well, in Chapter 5 we turn to the role of a member of parliament today, i.e., why he is elected. Earlier in Chapter 2 we discussed the protection needed for the fulfillment of that role. We now turn to what is happening in the European Parliament.

---

[*] <u>Immunités parlementaires ou impunité de parlementaire</u>, Hervé Issar, 20 Revue française de droit constitutionnel, 1994, p. 675. It is interesting to note that Holland is presently the only continental European country whose Members of Parliament since 1884, are not 'inviolable' beyond the proceedings of their parliament. See also Patrick Fraisseix at end note 52 for another comprehensive review of the position in France.

Chapter 4
The European Parliament[*]

The European Parliament, an admirable and courageous attempt to create unity amidst diversity following the ravages of World War II, is an ongoing experiment in democratic federalism of sorts. It is part of the institution-building that seeks to form existing nation-states into a pluralistic, multi-faceted community of communities. This ongoing complex experiment requires ongoing legal fine-tuning of the European Parliament. Fortunately, our concern is limited to the claim of parliamentary inviolability the European Parliament makes for its members.

The European Community Treaty of April 8, 1965, known as the Merger Treaty, established a single council and a single Commission of the European Communities. The Treaty provides that the members of the European Parliament shall enjoy in the territories of the Member States the privileges and immunities necessary for the performance of their tasks, under conditions set forth in the Protocol on the Privileges and Immunities of the European Communities (the "Protocol") annexed to the Merger Treaty. Articles 9 and 10 of the Protocol set out what are called the privileges and immunities of members of the European Parliament. Here lies the basis

---

[*] For what follows I rely mainly on the Internal Study of the European Parliament's Parliamentary Immunity in the European Parliament 2005, and Rules on Parliamentary Immunity in the European Parliament and the Member States of the European Union, 2001.

of the claim to parliamentary inviolability, i.e., protection from the criminal process.

Article 9

Members of the European Parliament shall not be subject to any form of inquiry, detention or legal proceedings in respect of opinions expressed or votes cast by them in the performance of their duties.

Article 10

During the sessions of the European Parliament its Members shall enjoy:

(a) in the territory of their own State, the immunities accorded to members of their parliament.

(b) in the territory of any other Member State, immunity from any measure of detention and from legal proceedings.

Immunity shall likewise apply to Members while they are traveling to and from the place of meeting of the European Parliament.

Immunity cannot be claimed when a Member is found in the act of committing an offence and shall not prevent the European Parliament from exercising its right to waive the immunity of one of its Members.

Article 9 appears to pose no problem. It seems equivalent to what the British parliamentary system understands by parliamentary privilege or immunity: the freedom of a member of parliament to speak and vote in parliamentary proceedings on all matters controversial without fear of legal consequences.

But a problem does exist. The expression "in the performance of their duties" requires interpretation. The

European Parliament wrestles with this, as we shall discuss later on. Let it suffice for now to note that Article 9 intends to protect a member's freedom to perform his duties subject only to the procedural rules and the rules of proper conduct (parliamentary etiquette, so to speak) that are wholly internal to and governed by Parliament itself, without interventions by any higher outside authority. Parliament is master of its own internal house, procedures, and good manners.

Article 10, however, on its face alone, raises huge problems that give rise to what Hervé Issar, author of <u>Immunités parlementaires ou impunité de parlementaire</u>, 20 revue française de droit constitutional 1994, calls a "hybrid right"[*].[54] It does so, as Issar well explains, by referring back to the national provisions governing parliamentary inviolability, instead of establishing a specific European parliamentary inviolability.

In Issar's words:[55]

> Article 10 'n'instaure pas un régime spécifique de l'inviolabilité du parlementaire européen mais renvoie au droit national dans le cas où les poursuites auraient été engagées sur le territoire de l'État dont le député est le représentant. Il n'y a donc pas, actuellement, un mais seize régimes différents d'inviolabilité des susceptibles d'être invoques au niveau communautaire. Dans le cas où un député européen est poursuivi par une juridiction de son pays d'origine il y a lieu d'appliquer les règles nationales relatives à l'immunité qui protége ses homologues nationaux. Mais, si le même député européen commet un même acte délictueux sur le territoire d'un autre État de la Communauté, c'est le régime de 'l'immunité communautaire défini à l'article 10-1b qui lui sera alors appliqué. Ainsi, un député européen de nationalité britannique, élu au Royaume-Uni, poursuivi pour homicide par les

---

[*]   « C'est donc un droit hybride qui continue, aujourd'hui, à s'appliquer en matière d'inviolabilité du parlementaire européen. » Issar, Ibid., p. 680.

tribunaux anglais, sera protégé comme le serait son homologue de la chambre des Communes, c'est-à-dire qu'il sera immédiatement poursuivi. Mais un député français qui commettrait les mêmes exactions sur le territoire britannique bénéficiera de l'application de l'article 10-1b et ne pourra donc être arrêté ou poursuivi sans que le Parlement européen ait préalablement levé son immunité.

When Issar wrote, there were 16 different national regimes. Today these regimes number 26. As the Member States of the European Union increase, the "hybrid right" expands rather than contracts.

The need for paragraph (a) of Article 10 made some sense in 1965 when the national parliaments appointed delegates to the Single Assembly of the European Community. Each individual member state laid down its own procedure for such appointments. But in 1976 all this changed with the election of members to the European Parliament by direct vote of the people of the Member States. However, instead of amending or repealing Article 10, the Parliament reaffirmed the April 1965 Protocol on Privileges and Immunities. Thus, during sessions of the European Parliament, its members elected directly by the people and not appointed as delegates of national parliaments, do not enjoy a specific European parliamentary inviolability, as Issar well expresses.

Consider the following example. A member of the European Parliament from England enjoys in England only the immunities recognized by the British Parliament. If he commits a crime in England, he must submit to the criminal process. If he commits a crime in another member country, he can claim European parliamentary inviolability. However, a member of the European Parliament from Belgium or France can claim European parliamentary inviolability for a crime committed in England. The Belgian or French member cannot be subjected to the criminal process in England while the English member feels the full force of that criminal process.

The European Parliament has yet to come to terms with and resolve this problem. Instead, it is building its own rules, what we may call a body of case law arising from decisions made on requests to it to waive parliamentary inviolability. It seems chimeric to hope that such rules will eventually bring about a coherent system of European parliamentary immunity that will stand on its own and not depend on the divergent laws, customs, procedures, and practices of the national parliaments.

Although the European Parliament seems to have developed a consistent practice to waive immunity, it knows the present system of privileges and immunities is gravely flawed. The system is a recipe for trouble. The European Parliament noticed this in 1985 when a <u>Memorandum on the Parliamentary Privileges in the European Communities</u> (Memorandum) by the Direction Générale de la Recherche et de la Documentation pointed out that "Members of Parliament enjoyed a status which differed according to their nationalities, as their national legislation differed in the degree of immunity afforded to Members." The protection against legal proceedings varies among Member States, as the Memorandum explains:

> 'Protection against criminal proceedings exists in Belgium, Denmark, Germany, France, Italy, Luxemburg; protection against civil proceedings exist in the U.K. In Ireland and in the Netherlands, protection is restricted to parliamentary activities of a Member'.

The same Memorandum shows that the European Parliament submitted proposals to amend the existing Protocol, citing as one of its reasons the following:

Since the exercise of an MEP's mandate is not and cannot be restricted to the territory of one Member State, the protection against criminal proceedings should not vary according to the place, where the Member happens to be. It should be identical throughout the Community, thus establishing a maximum of legal clarity.

Already now, a Community standard exists pursuant to Article 10, paragraph b) of the Protocol, as long as a Member is not in his country of origin.

In 2001, the European Centre for Parliamentary Research and Documentation (ECPRD) produced <u>Rules on Parliamentary Immunity in the European Parliament and the Member States of the European Union</u> (European Rules). Here we learn that the actual practice of waiving immunity is not as consistent as first appeared. The ECPRD acknowledged its debt to Marilio Crespo Allen's comprehensive European Parliament working paper entitled <u>Parliamentary Immunity in the Member States of the European Union and the European Parliament,</u> which was published in 1999. Allen's work is the basis for the 2001 ECPRD Rules.

The European Parliament sought to explain the discrepancies in its actual practice by noting the different factors of an "institutional, political and cultural nature", apart from legal regulations and jurisprudence, which the author of the working paper stressed and said must be taken into consideration. Although this made it difficult to present clear conclusions or trends, the author observed that, "It can be seen that the number of requests for the waiving of parliamentary immunity (or the suspension of detention or judicial proceedings) is substantially higher in some Member States (e.g. Italy, Greece) than in others (e.g. France, Denmark, Finland and Sweden)."

The European Rules note that a few other simple observations (Marilio Crispo Allen) can be made:

> In some parliaments there is a clear predominance of rejected requests relating to cases of waiving of immunity, which could indicate a broader interpretation of this concept (e.g. the Portuguese Assembly of the Republic, the Greek Chamber of Deputies), while in others the reverse is found (e.g. the Bundestag); in manycases, however, it is impossible to make out a clear and continual preponderance of accepted or rejected requests from the data supplied.
>
> Among the guiding principles used by the various parliaments as a basis for their decisions to refuse requests for the waiving of parliamentary immunity we find, in particular, the following:
>
> - verification of the existence of definite signs that the purpose of the criminal proceedings is to unfairly persecute the Member of Parliament and to threaten his freedom and independence in carrying out his mandate;
> - the political nature of the facts considered criminal;
> - the lack of seriousness of the facts or the obvious lack of grounds for the accusation.
>
> In contrast, the waiving of immunity has been based in particular on the 'serious, sincere and loyal' nature of the requests submitted and on the particular gravity or nature of the criminal offences imputed (such as when they involve an element of ostensible public scandal or their urgent evaluation in court is necessary, owing to the fact that the reputation of the parliamentary institution itself or the basic rights of third parties are involved), or else its purpose has been to enable all necessary investigative measures to be taken on the understanding that the judicial proceedings must be conducted in such a way

that they will not interfere with the discharge of parliamentary office.

Some parliaments have mentioned their right to grant requests to waive inviolability only in part, for instance by deciding on a case-by-case basis to refuse or authorise restrictions on freedom on which authorisation has been sought (France) or by giving permission for a Member to be, say, committed for trial but not arrested (Belgium).

Christian Kopetski, Department of Public Law, University of Austria, reminds us that the expressions, "political activities" and "political context" give rise to great difficulties when requests to waive a member's immunity, i.e., inviolability, are made. He also reminds us that, "for one thing, there is by no means unanimity of opinion as to what is meant by 'political context'... Secondly, there is the question of what consequences ought to arise out of an acceptance of the concept of a 'political context'. There are not a few prominent politicians and lawyers who take the standpoint that the law does not empower Parliament to lift a Member's immunity if the offence took place in a 'political context'."[56]

It may help to contrast the Canadian scene with that of the European Parliament in this manner. In 1994 a Canadian M.P. was sentenced to 14 days in prison for defying an order of the Supreme Court of British Columbia prohibiting anyone from interfering with loggers going to work in Clayoquot Sound on western Vancouver Island. According to the expanded notion of the European Parliament, he may have been engaged in "political activity". But any reasonably-minded person knows that it was not only beyond a proceeding in parliament but also beyond any political mandate that the M.P. had. This raises the question, what is the mandate of any M.P. in any part of the world in the twenty-first century. Is not a member of parliament elected to speak freely in parliament about abuses and controversial topics? Should he not be treated in the same way as his constituents, i.e. such that he and they are on a level playing field when they are both outside parliament?

Let us summarize briefly.

First, Article 9 contains no time limitation such as Article 10 expresses with the qualification: "during the sessions of the European Parliament". In this sense, Article 9 expresses the unqualified or absolute privilege and immunity of members of the European Parliament in the performance of their duties. On its face, therefore, Article 9 raises two questions upon which opinion is divided: When does one become and cease to be a member? More importantly, what constitutes "performance of their duties"?

Second, Article 10 is deeply problematic in that it gives rise to the issue of inviolability and the waiving of such inviolability by the European Parliament.

Third, beyond reasonable doubt, the inviolability-waiving process is highly subjective, replete with the absurdities and inconsistencies, the foibles and follies of human nature. This is evidenced by the procedure and practice of the European Parliament, by studies, reports, and especially the very existence of what Hervé Issar calls a "hybrid right": a combination of the referral back to national laws, with the practice and procedure of the European Parliament, which is the chief reason for the tangled tale of the inviolability-waiving process.

Fourth, the intended purpose of Articles 9 and 10 is the protection of the European Parliament as an institution and not the protection of its members.

Fifth, paragraph (a) of Article 10 may have been justified when national parliaments appointed delegates, but it lost such justification with the election of members to the European Parliament by direct vote of the people.

A further problem arises with the expressions "legal proceedings" in paragraph (b) of Article 10 of the Protocol. This was once restricted to criminal proceedings which was the better opinion. Today, however, the European Parliament inclines toward a less restrictive interpretation that would include certain types of civil proceedings that appear punitive. (Punitive damages are those claimed in a civil action that are clearly intended to deter the individual from repeating the act complained of. They may also serve to deter other possible imitators.) The European Parliament has in recent years upheld immunity in certain civil actions of this sort. Thus it appears that inviolability is being enlarged rather than diminished.

Article 10 of the Protocol, then, is what gives rise to the "hybrid right". The convoluted interpretations of this provision by the European Parliament would baffle the best Philadelphia lawyer. Analysis of these interpretative decisions is beyond the scope of this book. Article 9, more closely approximating parliamentary privilege or immunity in the British parliamentary system, presents less difficulty. With respect to our first question above, when does one begin and cease to be a member of the European Parliament, the answer seems to be, (for purposes of immunity, at least), from the moment one is declared elected until the end of one's term of office. This view, however, is not shared by all.

Article 9 of the Protocol states that a member of the European Parliament may not be subject to any legal proceedings in respect of opinions expressed "in the performance of their duties". If this means whether inside Parliament or not, and since article 10 provides protection from legal proceedings, it seems the member may rail to his heart's content in the midst of his electors and opponents, who may retaliate only within the law of the land for the unelected. Hardly upholding the principle of equality before the law.

What constitutes "in the performance of their duties", remains problematic. Although Article 9 clearly applies only to "opinions expressed or votes cast" by members, the unresolved issue remains whether the performance of duties extends beyond the proceedings of the sessions of the European Parliament.

A sense of the approach taken is set out in this excerpt from a report in 2006 on a proposal for a European Parliament decision on the request for a waiver of the immunity (inviolability) of a German member of the European Parliament:

> Immunity is intended to protect the freedom which Members have to express their opinion and engage in political debate. The committee responsible for dealing with the matter has therefore always proceeded according to the basic principle that whenever incriminated actions fall under the heading of, or are related directly to, a Member's political activity, immunity is not waived.
>
> Cases in the above category include, for example, those in which opinions deemed to form part of a Member's political activity are expressed during demonstrations, at public rallies, in political publications, in the press, in a book, on television, through the act of signing a political tract, or even before a court of law.
>
> In addition to this principle, there are other considerations which militate in favour of or against waiver of immunity, in particular the "fumus

persecutionis"*, that is to say, the presumption that criminal proceedings stem from an intention to damage a Member's political activity. As indicated in the explanatory statement contained in the Donnez report, the concept of "fumus persecutionis" means essentially that immunity is not waived when it is suspected that criminal proceedings are intended at bottom to undermine the political activity of the Member concerned. [57]

The answer may be found when in 1986, the Inter-Parliamentary Union stated in its <u>Corporate Reference Compendium</u> that "immunities relate primarily to the exercise of parliamentary duties". This supports the thrust of my thesis that parliamentary inviolability should be abolished especially as one looks to the development of the rule of law and parliamentary institutions in the twenty-first century.

Member States of the European Union and members of the European Parliament say they adhere to the 1950 <u>Rome Convention for the Protection of Human Rights and Fundamental Freedoms,</u> in which the preamble affirms "that they have a common heritage…the Rule of law".

Yet, rather than stiffen its spine and reject parliamentary inviolability, the European Parliament continues to engage in

---

* <u>Fumus persecutionis</u> is a presumption that the criminal proceedings are intended to prejudice the member's political activities. Anonymous information at the basis of a preliminary investigation or delay in making the request to waive parliamentary inviolability, may give rise to such presumption. Still, it is only a presumption. For instance, the inquiry that led in France to National Assembly member Alain Juppé's prosecution was the result of a 'dénonciation anonyme'. Juppé, a former prime minster of France, at the time also mayor of Bordeaux, a regional councilor, and head of President Chirac's Union for Popular Movement (UMP) party. In January 2004, Juppé was convicted of illegally financing Chirac's ruling party by paying party officials out of funds from Paris City Hall between 1988 and 1995, when he was municipal financial director and Chirac was mayor. And, as we know, many if not most criminal investigations begin with information from someone, anonymous or not.

sometimes bizarre interpretations of the nature and scope of inviolability. It refuses to engage in a free, reasoned, responsible, and open debate on parliamentary inviolability. Issar seems to read the situation correctly (in 1994) when he explains why such debate will not happen soon:

> Les réticences britanniques, l'intense activité du Conseil et la crise politico-institutionnelle que traverse actuellement l'Europe communautaire ne permettant cependant pas de penser qu'un débat, nécessairement passionnel, sur l'immunité parlementaire puisse rapidement être inscrit à l'ordre du jour du Conseil.[58]

The problem, of course, does not arise in a system that rejects inviolability and affirms that parliamentary immunity suffices for the protection of Parliament as a vibrant institution in a modern, liberal, democratic state. Anyone who doubts this need but look to the time-tested experience of the British Parliament and its offshoots, and of the Congress of the U.S.A. and the legislatures of its fifty states.

In the European Parliament today there are 26 sovereign member states of the European Union. Each has its own scheme of parliamentary immunity within its national territory. As the European Parliament must look to these various national regimes in considering requests for waiver of immunity, there sometime arises a byzantine quality to the process and practice.

As example, take the case of the 2001 request by Spanish authorities to have the European Parliament waive the immunity of Italy's conservative opposition leader Silvio Berlusconi. The authorities made the request to help a tax-fraud investigation of a Spanish TV station in which Berlusconi had a substantial stake. The European Parliament simply took no action. The Spanish Leader of the Socialist group in the European Parliament sent a letter to the President of the Parliament demanding an explanation. The President defended the inaction on grounds of procedural error by the Spanish investigating magistrate who initiated the request. The Associated Press reported the affair as follows:

> From Brussels, it was reported that the President of the European Parliament, Nicole Fontaine,... defended the assembly's lack of response to a Spanish request to lift the parliamentary immunity of Italy's conservative opposition leader Silvio Berlusconi... Fontaine said there were doubts that Spanish authorities had followed the correct procedures when they lodged the request last July to help a tax-fraud probe of a Spanish TV station in which the Italian media magnate and ex-premier had a big stake. Fontaine was responding to a letter Tuesday from Enrique Baron, Spanish leader of the Socialist group in the Parliament, who demanded that she explain the lack of action in the case. Fontaine, a French conservative, said Spain's Supreme Court had lodged the request directly with the European Parliament's delegation in Madrid, without passing by the Spanish government's mission to the European Union. 'This resulted in a doubt about whether we could receive it,' Fontaine's statement said. 'The precautionary initiative... to obtain clarification from the Spanish authorities was therefore perfectly founded.'... Spain made the request to lift the immunity of Berlusconi as part of an investigation of a suspected 5 billion peseta (dlrs 28 million) tax fraud case at Telecinco, one of Spain's private television channels.... The request came on the initiative of investigation magistrate, Baltasar Garzon, who came to international prominence with his attempt to secure the extradition to Spain of Chilean former dictator Augusto Pinochet. Berlusconi won a seat in 1998 elections to the 626-member European Parliament and thus obtained immunity from

prosecution and investigation in all 15 countries of the European Union.[*]

It seems clear, however, to an outsider looking in, that attempt to find an autonomous notion of parliamentary immunity for the European Parliament as distinct from immunity in the Member States will always end up in a cul-de-sac until the European Parliament faces head-on in open debate the issue of inviolability.

Until then, interpretations of Article 10 of the Protocol will continue to produce unequal treatment of the members of the European Parliament. In the territory of their own state, the immunities accorded to members of their parliaments, in the territory of any other state, immunity from any measure of detention from legal proceedings. As the Parliament must look to various national regimes, their laws, practices, and procedures, its task of interpretation is fraught with misunderstanding, mistake, misjudgment, and delay. Such interpretation will increase in nebulosity as factors of an «institutional, political, and cultural nature» are introduced to justify its decisions. And all the while, such task of interpretation will consume inordinate time, energy, and effort, and will adversely impact the genuine work of the European Parliament as a parliament.

As the Internal Study of Parliamentary in the European Parliament in 2005 put it: This situation also has an adverse impact on Parliament's own work, since it obliges Parliament, in connection with each request for the waiver of parliamentary immunity, to consider the relevant national rules governing immunity and the related procedures. This

---

[*] Brussels, 21 February 2001, Associated Press Newswires. See further, the Annex to the 2005 Internal Study referred to earlier, for the Table of Decisions regarding requests for waiver of parliamentary immunity of members of the E.P.

may lead to decision- making errors in interpretation and even the misapplication of the relevant rules.

It seems beyond reasonable doubt that the best way to develop a genuine European Parliament immunity, autonomous and non-dependent on Member-State variations, is to eliminate inviolability. The integrity of that parliamentary institution does not require it.

The next chapter develops arguments for the abolition of parliamentary inviolability <u>tout court</u>. The European Parliament and its Member States would help immensely by leading the way.

Chapter 5
Abolition of Inviolability

Our study so far has shown how the different historical developments in England and continental Europe brought about two different parliamentary regimes. Before embarking on a critical assessment of parliamentary inviolability, let us now consider what the function of a national parliament is and why a member is elected.

The function of a national parliament in a modern-day democracy is to establish a legitimate government through the electoral process and to make a government work. This means that it gives the government the authority, the funds, and the other resources necessary for governing the country by legislation and policy making. It also means that a national parliament acts like a watchdog over the government -to ensure that it behaves, to provide political communications, and when needed to make available an alternative government, i.e. to enable the opposition to present its case to the public and become a credible choice to replace the party in power.

A member of parliament is therefore elected to act on behalf of constituents <u>but</u> within the function of a national parliament.

There lies the daily reality of the many roles a member in fact plays: constituency representative and ombudsman; orator and law-maker; policy-maker and watchdog over the government and bureaucracy; loyal party member and sensitive family member. These are huge demands on any human being, who cannot hope to play all these roles adequately.

In a democratic political system of representative and responsible government, most members of parliament are activist, talkative, and run from meeting to meeting. But only a few of these meetings are of committees of parliament. Most meetings are with constituents, with groups wanting to bend his or her ear on some matter of policy or administration, with other members, with journalists, civil servants, groups from foreign countries, and with many of the innumerable groups and individuals whose interests and concerns are affected by government and politics. The job is people-oriented, 'involving talking about and listening to ideas, proposals, and complaints; reconciling opposing viewpoints; explaining the party or government policy to citizens, and citizens' views to the party and the government; getting the government to act on problems of constituents; and examining how the government uses or abuses the power it exercises on behalf of the people.[59]

The tremendous range of work a member must engage in is often not appreciated by the general public. As Henry J. Schmandt and Paul G. Steinbicker of St. Louis University stated in their book Fundamentals of Government in connection with a member of the U.S. Congress:

> The lawmaker – contrary to popular belief – must spend long and difficult hours at his work: in committee meetings, on the floor of the house, in conferences, in greeting friends and delegations from his district, in serving as an errand boy for his constituents who will request information ranging from the proper breeding of swine to the reasons for an army court-martial of a boy from his district, in studying bills and reports and keeping up with current affairs, in filling speaking and social engagements, and in answering the large daily mail which is the

lot of most congressmen. During the course of his term, he is likely to be accused of corruption, of nepotism, of being a lackey of big business or a mouthpiece of labor, and of seeking special privileges for his friends. Unless he can learn to take abuse and criticism in stride, his life will be an unhappy one, for no matter what he does or what stand he takes on a controversial measure, he is certain to make enemies. Finally, he will be subject to pressure from all sides – from his party leaders, from politicians at home, from lobbyists, from individuals and groups in his district, from his colleagues in the legislature, and from numerous other sources.[60]

However, while a member has all these functions because he is elected to serve his electors in parliament, he is immune only when he is functioning in parliament. Is it right that the state pursue only the citizen and not the member when, side by side, they both break the law while taking part together in a public demonstration? If a member of parliament and a friend who is not a member take part together in a public political parade and the friend (encouraged, i.e. aided and abetted, by the member who is equally involved in the illegal activity but not in flagrante delicto) deliberately causes injury to a person or damage to property, why should the friend be arrested and be subject to prosecution and detention but not the member (unless his parliament gives consent)? Does this not fly in the face of the rule of law and the principle of equality before the law?

The member's activities outside parliament provide him or her with the material information to expose and denounce abuses by means of the freedom of speech he or she enjoys while taking part in a proceeding of parliament. The persistent questions naturally assert themselves: Why does a member of parliament or of a national assembly anywhere on planet earth require parliamentary inviolability (in the continental European sense as immunity from the normal criminal process) in order to function completely and freely as a member of the national parliament or of the European Parliament on behalf of constituents? Why is parliamentary <u>immunity</u> (In the British-based sense that excludes inviolability) not sufficient? Can we still claim as valid the historical reasons giving rise to the different development in continental Europe and beyond? Can parliamentary inviolability be justified in the twenty-first century world?

If it can be, it means that humankind has failed in providing the rule of law in those jurisdictions. Abolishing parliamentary inviolability is a way to move the rule of law and good governance forward.

Now let us discuss why today the claim to parliamentary inviolability is not only outdated but is repugnant to the rule of law and to good governance. Recall that the privilege of inviolability was first claimed for members of the Revolutionary Assembly on June 23, 1789, by Mirabeau. Perhaps at that time, in that particular political climate, the claim may not have been unreasonable given "la puissance des baïonnettes," monarchical absolutism, les lettres de cachet, and aristocratic privileges in France. But from such admission of possible justification at that time in that place, one can hardly infer its reasonableness today in the twenty-first century.

With Mirabeau's words came the earliest form of inviolability as set forth that same historic day in Article V of the Declaration of the French National Assembly. In his *Les constitutions de la France*, Adolphe Faustin Hélie explains:

> L'Assemblée nationale déclare que la personne de chacun des députés est inviolable; que tous particuliers, toute corporation, tribunal, cour ou commission, qui oseraient, pendant ou après la présente session, poursuivre, rechercher, arrêter ou faire arrêter, détenir, ou faire détenir un député pour raison d'aucune proposition, avis, opinion ou

discours par lui fait aux États-Généraux, de même que toutes personnes qui prêteraient leur ministère à aucun desdits attentats, de quelque part qu'ils fussent ordonnés, sont infâmes et traîtres envers la nation, et coupables de crime capital. L'Assemblée nationale arrête que, dans les cas susdits, elle prendra toutes les mesures nécessaires pour faire rechercher, poursuivre et punir ceux qui en seront les auteurs, instigateurs ou exécuteurs.[*]

---

[*] 'La séance royale eut lieu le 23 juin. Louis XVI y déclara que la constitution de la majorité des députés en Assemblée nationale était nulle, et que les États-Généraux resteraient divisés en trois ordres; il fit ensuite donner lecture d'une déclaration détaillée des réformes qu'il consentait et dans laquelle il reconnaissait aux États-Généraux avec quelques améliorations le pouvoir dont ils avaient jouis autrefois. Ainsi le Roi se prononçait contre la presque unanimité de la nation, qui voulait une nouvelle constitution conforme à l'état actuel de la France, et dont le désir était juste et légitime. Le bon droit était du côté de l'Assemblée nationale. Après la séance royale, tous les députés qui avaient adhéré aux déclarations des 17 et 20 juin, demeurèrent dans la salle, malgré le commandement royal qui prescrivait de ne plus délibérer que par ordre. L'Assemblée, après la réplique célèbre de Mirabeau au maître des cérémonies, vota d'abord à l'unanimité le maintien des deux déclarations précédentes, et ensuite, sur la motion de Mirabeau par 493 voix contre 34, la déclaration ci-dessus qui les confirme. La veille de cette séance, le 22 juin, l'Assemblée s'était réunie dans l'église cathédrale de Saint-Louis. La majorité de l'ordre du clergé, qui avait vote le 19 juin par 145 voix contre 139 la réunion au tiers, y était venue siéger dans l'Assemblée. Le même jour deux députés de la noblesse avaient abandonné leur corps et étaient venus aussi prendre place. Le 24, lendemain de la séance royale, malgré l'ordre que le gouvernement n'était pas assez fort pour faire exécuter, l'Assemblée nationale tint séance; 151 députés du clergé étaient présents, et ce même jour, 47 députés de la noblesse se rendirent dans l'Assemblée et y prirent leur siège. Ainsi ce furent la majorité du clergé et une minorité de la noblesse qui refusèrent d'obéir à l'ordre royal du 23 juin. Un tel mouvement était irrésistible non moins que juste. Le Roi céda, et le 27 juin il sutorisa les membres du clergé et de la nobles encore dissidents à se réunir à l'Assemblée nationale. Le pouvoir constituant de l'Assemblée fut ainsi reconnu, après une courte lutte.' Commentaire sur l'Article V, Déclaration de l'assemblée nationale sur l'inviolabilité des députés. M. Faustin-Adolphe Hélie, *Les constitutions de la France*, avec un commentaire par M. Paris, A. Marescq ainé, Librarie-Éditeur, 1875.

Two years later, there followed the earliest legislated form of parliamentary inviolability in Articles 7 and 8 of the French Constitution of 1791:

> Article 7 – Les représentants de la nation sont inviolables: ils ne pourront être recherchés, accusés ni jugés en aucun temps pour ce qu'ils auront dit, écrit ou fait dans l'exercice de leurs fonctions de représentants.

> Article 8 – Ils pourront, pour fait criminel, être saisis en flagrant délit, ou en vertu d'un mandat d'arrêt; mais il en sera donné avis, sans délai, au Corps législatif; et la poursuite ne pourra être continuée qu'après que le Corps législatif aura décidé qu'il y a lieu à accusation.

Nonetheless, their claimed inviolability as members of the National Assembly or National Convention did not save Danton or Robespierre from the Reign of Terror and the guillotine in 1794. One may ask, does it save others today in many countries where analogous circumstances of fear and retribution and tyranny may exist? These countries have modelled their claim to parliamentary inviolability on either these original Articles 7 and 8 of the French Constitution of 1791 or the form of the claim made at present (1995) in Article 26 of the Constitution of France, which states:

> No Member of Parliament can be prosecuted, sought, arrested, detained or tried because of opinions expressed, or votes cast in the exercise of their functions.

> No Member of Parliament can be subjects in a criminal or correctional matter, of an arrest or of any other measure [which] deprives or restricts liberty, except with the authorization of the Bureau of the Assembly of which he [she] is a member. This authorization is not required, in case of a crime or misdemeanour of final conviction.

The detention, the measures which deprive or restrict the liberty or the prosecution of a member of Parliament are suspended for the duration if the session of the Assembly, of which he [she] is a part, so requests.[*]

In other words, the only possible excuse for the claim to parliamentary inviolability might be in the so-called underdeveloped or developing countries or "post dictator" countries where circumstances analogous to "la puissance des baïonnettes" may be said to exist under governments led by tyrants by means of rule <u>by</u> law rather than rule *of* law. The reader may recall that the expression 'rule <u>by</u> law' connotes that the law merely serves the power of the state whereas 'rule <u>of</u> law' connotes that law limits the power of the state.

It was this fear of the executive, which was ubiquitous on the continent, that gave rise to the principle whereby responsibility for establishing whether proceedings are fair and well-founded and not attributable to persecution on political or personal grounds lies with a committee of the parliament. But neither in France nor in the European Parliament nor in any other so-called developed country can the claim today be reasonably asserted. Nor can it really be justified in other countries. The possible excuse suggested above is a mere excuse for a de facto state of affairs in search of justification (and no doubt foreign assistance).

---

[*] This attempt at reform did not impress everyone. Patrick Frasseix wrote, 'La loi constitutionnelle du 4 août 1995, s'insérant dans le cadre du prurit réformateur agitant les constituants depuis 1992, est venue réviser les règles de l'inviolabilité parlementaire... d'autre part pour limiter les modalités de cette protection de plus en plus mal perçue par l'opinion publique, encline à l'assimiler à autant de subterfuges dilatoires faisant échapper les élus dépositaires de la souveraineté nationale des objurgations judiciaires. (Revue Française de Droit Constitutionel, v. 39, p. 502, 1999). For the exercise in France see <u>Chronique Constitutionnelle Française</u> in <u>Revue Française d'Études Constitutionnelles et Critiques</u> 1977 to the present under headings <u>Immunités parlementaires, Inviolabilité, Levée de l'immunité.</u>

The Inter-parliamentary Centre for Parliamentary Documentation produced in 1986 a useful Comparative Reference Compendium, 1986, 2nd Vol., in which 83 of the 142 parliaments of sovereign states across the world had responded to the questionnaire. The Compendium stated:

> The objective of parliamentary immunities is to protect Members of Parliament from legal actions by the Government or by private persons. Historically, their purpose was to safeguard the precarious position of elected assemblies against powerful Governments. While their original purpose has considerably changed, they are, nonetheless, still justifiable in the contemporary world as their existence also facilitates the smooth running and complete independence of Parliament.

It went on to state, "for this reason, immunities relate primarily to the exercise of *parliamentary* duties", which, it is suggested, goes a long way to support the thrust of this present inquiry.

If the reader accepts the arguments that now follow, he or she may agree with the assertion that parliamentary inviolability today is per se odious and must be abolished as inimical to good governance because it is inimical to (1) the separation of powers; (2) the rule of law and equality before the law; (3) prosecutorial discretion; (4) independence of the judiciary; and (5) the role of a member of parliament. These considerations overlap and cumulatively demonstrate why parliamentary inviolability must be jettisoned. Let us, however, discuss them seriatim to try to get a better grasp of the point I am trying to make.

The Separation of Powers

Recall the words of Pym (see Endnote 30) in the seventeenth century, which take on greater significance today.

The privileges of Parliament were not given for the ornament or advantage of those who are the members of Parliament. They have a real use and efficacy towards that which is the end of Parliaments. We are free from suits that we may the more entirely addict ourselves to the public services; we have liberty of speech that our counsels may not be corrupted with fear, or our judgments perverted with self respects. Those three great faculties and functions of Parliament, the legislative, judiciary, and consiliary power, cannot be well exercised without such privileges as these. The wisdom of our laws, the faithfulness of our counsels, the righteousness of our judgments, can hardly be kept pure and untainted if they proceed from distracted and restrained minds. These powers of Parliament are to the body politic as the rational faculties of the soul to a man: that which keeps all the parts of the Commonwealth in frame and temper ought to be most carefully preserved in that freedom, vigour and activity which belongs to itself.

Recall also the role of a modern-day constitution. It is an arrangement of political offices that designates the powers of the various offices and their responsibilities. Its most important characteristic is that <u>those who govern do not do so by power vested in them personally but by the power vested in the office</u>. Thus a constitutional government is a government of laws and not of men.

From the time of Montesquieu's masterpiece l'<u>Esprit des lois</u> (1748),* in which he examined the three types of government (republic, monarchy, and despotism), it has

---

* <u>L'Esprit des lois</u> was the product of 20 years work. It was attacked immediately and two years later Montesquieu responded to the attacks with his <u>Défence de L'Esprit des lois</u> (1750). All legislators, especially those of the European Parliament, might re-acquaint themselves with Montesquieu's masterpiece and his subsequent defence of it. Truth does not age.

become a commonplace of legal-political thought to affirm with that great jurist that governmental powers should be separated and balanced to guaranty individual rights and freedom.

Today a constitution is the fundamental law of a state. It fixes and defines the relations between legislative, judicial, and executive powers (parliament, the courts, the government). This sets the foundation for government, a <u>government of laws not of men</u>, a government whose power derives from the people for whom governments exist. Various theories of law, the sources of law, and the ultimate sources of authority, power, and government abound. I believe it to be a fair generalization today that the dynamic of the complexities of good governance rightly moves from an unstated assumption that the modern constitution is the legal basis of an ordered political society, that the three powers are separate though related, that the government is of laws and not of men, and that its power, expressed in the constitution, derives from the people.

Good governance requires wisdom, experience, and sound judgment about the complexities of contemporary living. It also requires that all the people including members of Parliament be subject to the same law, respect the same constitution, the same separation of powers. Parliamentary inviolability cannot be justified as a pretext for the proper functioning of parliament. It flies in the face of constitutional government and the separation of powers.[*]

---

[*] Thus it is said in France, 'les modalités de cette empiètement du pouvoir législatif sur le domaine réserve de l'autorité judiciaire semble néanmoins dérogé aux principes fondamentals de la séparation des pouvoirs.' (Patrick Fraisseix, p. 499)

The Rule of Law and Equality Before the Law

As we saw earlier, the rule of law is both an ideal and partial human achievement, an ongoing partially realized goal.[61] Here we emphasize one characteristic: it asserts that all persons are under the rule of law, both sovereign and subject, leaders and led. The words of the Honourable Charles L. Dubin, former chief justice of Ontario, bear repeating: "Over the centuries since the time of Aristotle people have sought to be governed not by the rules of a tyrant or of an unruly mob but by the rule of law, a law equally applicable to the powerful and the weak, the rich and the poor, without discrimination"[*]

Clearly, parliamentary inviolability claims special treatment for parliamentarians. It offends this characteristic of the rule of law: equality of all before the law. The Italian Constitution Court made this abundantly clear in its decision about the Berlusconi legislation.

And so, in the twenty-first century, as we attempt across the world to promote a human legal order grounded in modern constitutionalism and the rule of law, lawmakers above all should be in the forefront seeking abolition of parliamentary inviolability as an affront to the rule of law they claim to be upholding and promoting.

Chief Justice of Canada Mclachlin has said, "The rule of law is at the heart of our society: without it, there can be neither peace, nor order nor good government. The rule of law is directly dependent on the ability of the courts to enforce their process…"[62]

---

[*] In Italian court rooms, above the judge's bench, is displayed a ringing declaration: 'the law is equal for all'. . 3

Prosecutorial Discretion

In claiming inviolability, parliamentarians also claim the right to exercise prosecutorial discretion over their own. This ousting of normal executive prosecutorial discretion is a further affront. As with the separation of powers, it is a commonplace today that discretion to prosecute lies with those responsible for the administration of justice and the implementation of the criminal law of the state. Prosecutorial authority lies with the executive, not the legislative branch of government. By insisting that parliamentary inviolability be retained, parliamentarians usurp a role that is not theirs, encourage clashes with the prosecutorial authority, and publicly express a want of confidence not only in the executive but also in the judiciary. A clear example of the latter, (and of the defence of parliamentary inviolability) occurred in France following the conviction of parliamentarian Alain Juppé, as reported in The Times of London by Charles Bremner:

> President Chirac challenged France's judges yesterday when he publicly threw his weight behind Alain Juppé, the political lieutenant whose conviction on corruption charges has seriously shaken the French leader.... The head of state, who is the guarantor of the judicial system, angered the judges by appearing to reject Juppé's conviction, fuelling the fire by depicting the judges as politically biased.... The unions of investigating and bench judges condemned the way in which M. Chirac, Jean-Pierre Raffarin, the Prime Minister, and their centre-right camp were questioning the workings of justice. The Union of Judges, the main professional association, called on the political world to stop criticizing the judiciary. "This is a matter that involves the stability of national institutions and democracy in general. Justice and Judges must not be used as weapons in a politician's battle."... The row has all the hallmarks of the political meddling in the justice system that stained France's image in an earlier era.[63]

The day before, on February 2, 2004, Hervé Gattegno reported in <u>Le Monde</u> that Jean-Pierre Raffarin "a fait part de 'sa surprise' ajoutant : "Le service de la France et des français a besoin d'Alain Juppé". L'avocat de M. Juppé, Me Francis Szpiner, s'en est pris à 'la justice, qui veut se mettre au-dessus de la politique'. Dans leur édition du Samedi, 31 janvier, Libération et le Parisien font état de 'menace' sur les juges."[64]

However Patrick Fraisseix in <u>Revue Française de Droit Constitutionel 1999</u>, v.39 expresses a different view, which appears closer to the mark :

> Sans nier l'évidence d'une vieille judiciaire renforcée et de sanctions plus fréquente que subsissent les parlementaires ces derniers temps, toute conclusion manichéenne dénonçant l'ombre portée sournoise et tyrannique des juges ne paraît guère convaincante... La Res publica n'est toujours pas devenue l'orage des juges, le 'Gouvernement des juges' ne revèt encore aucune réalité crédile.
> (at p.510)

The exercise of prosecutorial discretion by parliamentarians smacks of interfering with and obstructing the judical process and, yes, it smacks also of elitism. It is the independent prosecutorial discretion along with the developed rules governing the circumstances concerning when the person may be released on bail and the conditions to be attached that are thus thwarted. Philip Stenning, author of <u>Appearing for the Crown, A Legal and Historical Review of Criminal Prosecutorial Authority in Canada</u>, A study conducted for the Law Reform Commission of Canada, 1986, puts his finger on the heart of the matter when he quotes John Edwards, (author of <u>the Law Offices of the Crown</u>, 1964):

> It is my contention that there exists a fundamental demarcation that needs to be constantly borne in mind when analyzing the application of the doctrine

of ministerial accountability in the area of policing and prosecutions. We begin with the proposition... that anything savouring of personal advancement or sympathy felt by an Attorney General, or Solicitor General towards a political colleague or supporter (or opponent) or which relates to the political fortune of his party and the government in power should not be countenanced if adherence to the principles of impartiality and integrity are to be publicly manifested. This does not mean that the Attorney General in the realm of prosecutions, or the Solicitor General in the area of policing, should not have regard to political considerations in the non-partisan interpretation of the term "politics". Thus, it might be thought that here are legitimate political grounds for taking into account such matters as the maintenance of ethnic groups, the maintenance of industrial peace and generally the interests of the public at large in deciding whether (or when) to initiate criminal proceedings or whether (and when) to terminate a prosecution that is in progress. All these broad political considerations, whether domestic or international in character, must be seen to involve the wider public interest that benefits the population at large rather than any single political group or factional interest. In my perception of the term, "partisan politics" has a much narrower focus and is designed to protect or advance the retention of constitutional power by the incumbent government and its political supporters. It is the intervention of political considerations in this latter sense that should have no place in the making of prosecutorial decisions...[65]

Independence of the Judiciary

An independent judiciary (supported by an independent bar) guards the separation of powers and the freedom of the citizenry, non-parliamentarians and parliamentarians alike. That judiciary determines whether the prosecutorial authority acted properly in arresting, detaining, obtaining a search or wiretap warrant against a member of parliament, or in charging a member with a criminal offence. The member need not be any more concerned than any other citizen that the rule of law will not prevail. If members of parliament insist that parliamentary inviolability need be retained, this means they publicly mistrust the judiciary and the executive branches, and they publicly proclaim a right to be on a pedestal above the ordinary citizen with regard to the criminal process. They thereby dishonour the meaning and role of a modern constitution that exists to govern the government and curb excessive governmental power through the separation of powers. Justice David Souter of the Supreme Court of the United States recounted in May 2009 what he called- "the most perfect statement" of an independent judiciary: "Because there has to be a safe place."*

The Role of a Member of Parliament

Recall that parliamentary inviolability is claimed by parliament as a body, for its proper functioning, and the member is elected to do parliamentary work and is provided with immunity in parliament. Now consider the following examples of what happens when legislators overstep their traditional role as law makers. These examples illustrate how, by pressing their claim beyond immunity to inviolability, and by replacing normal executive prosecutorial discretion with parliamentary prosecutorial discretion over their own, parliamentarians promote clashes among the holders of legislative, executive, and judicial powers, with consequent disrespect among them and dismay among the rest of us.

---

* (Washington Post. May 25, 2009)

In Italy we read in 2004 that "Berlusconi has been at the forefront of this campaign (of anti-corruption) periodically denouncing the judiciary in the most extreme terms."[66]

In France, as reported in Le Monde, "Dans leur édition du Samedi, 31 janvier, 2004 Libération et Le Parisien font état de 'menaces' sur les juges"[67] following the conviction of Alain Juppé.

In the Slovak Republic, we read that the Slovak parliament in 2001 voted at a closed meeting against stripping opposition deputy Gustav Krajci of his parliamentary immunity, thus rejecting a request from the investigator.[68]

Clearly, parliamentarians mistrust the executive power acting through the police or the office of the prosecutor, reject the integrity of the judiciary that oversees the correctness of each instance of prosecutorial discretion when an accused appears before the court, and claim for themselves an inviolability shared by no other citizen. They usurp for their own benefit such prosecutorial discretion. In so doing, parliamentarians deny the ability and integrity of both the prosecutor's office and the judiciary to differentiate between (a) genuine parliamentary immunity required for the proper functioning of parliament and (b) parliamentary inviolability which today is nothing but a discredited claim to escape the full force of the normal criminal process.

Canada presents two interesting scenarios that are à propos. One deals with a recent and serious flirtation with parliamentary inviolability. The other concerns a member of parliament charged with a criminal offence.

The serious flirtation occurred in 1990 in the Canadian House of Commons. It resulted from testimony given to a parliamentary committee in December 1989 by the Commissioner of the Royal Canadian Mounted Police (RCMP).

He told the Committee that the RCMP since 1985 had investigated over 30 cases involving Canadian parliamentarians, both those appointed to the Senate and those elected to the House of Commons. He added that there were, at the time he was testifying, about 15 ongoing investigations. Intense media coverage in effect launched the establishing of a parliamentary committee two days later.* This in turn resulted in a draft bill proposed by that committee to clarify the jurisdiction of the Commons' Board of Internal Economy.** The bill proposed to give the Board "exclusive authority" to determine the propriety of any use by members of money, goods, services, or premises made available for the carrying out of parliamentary and other functions. However it also proposed to prohibit any criminal process respecting such matters unless the Board had first been consulted. The proposed procedure in relation to the specified criminal processes would, in effect, establish a regime for federal parliamentarians that was quite different from that of other Canadians. Furthermore, if the determinations of the Board had been characterized as final or binding decisions, there would have been legal implications, since, the body would have been operating similarly to a court of law, making decisions about guilt or innocence and the rights of individuals.

---

* During 1989 there appeared to be an increasing number of police investigations involving parliamentarians, including a rise in the number of search warrants being executed on Parliament Hill. The criminal law applies throughout Canada except when the activity is part of a proceeding in Parliament, e.g. uttering a criminal libel during a debate in Parliament. A number of the matters being investigated related to the office budgets and services for the carrying out of parliamentary and other functions and duties of parliamentarians. These developments led to considerable concern on the part of some Members of Parliament.

** The Board, which is composed of the Speaker, Deputy Speaker and representatives of the political parties in the House, is responsible for the administration of internal affairs and the budgets of the House of Commons and its Members to act on all matters respecting money, goods, services, and premises made available to Members of the House of Commons.

While the draft bill proposed in effect to insulate members of the House of Commons from the criminal law of the land, yet there was hardly a murmur of discomfort at the committee. The evidence of the public sessions of the committee also does not reveal any dissenting advice from the senior advisor the house, the Clerk, regarding the draft bill's lack of historical integrity .The historical reality set out by John Hatsell in his <u>Precedents and Proceedings in the House of Commons</u>, 1818, is that even from the earliest times to 1628, there was not a single instance of a member claiming their privilege of parliament to withdraw himself from the criminal law of the land[*]. Thankfully the result of strong opposition from police authorities, the media,[70] the legal profession, and some parliamentarians, the original bill's mandatory provisions requiring a peace officer to seek an opinion from the Board were modified to provide that seeking such opinion was discretionary. The discretionary proposal in the bill, finally enacted as law, came before the courts in Ontario and Quebec when members of Parliament facing criminal charges sought to exclude the application of the Canadian <u>Criminal Code</u> to their fraud charges.

---

[*] In the well known English case of Bradlaugh v. Gossett in 1884, Lord Chief Justice Stephen said "I know of no authority for the proposition that an ordinary crime committed in the House of Commons would be withdrawn from the ordinary course of criminal justice. One of the leading authorities on the privilege of Parliament (Eliot's Case) contains matter on the point and shows how careful Parliament has been to avoid even the appearance of countenancing such a doctrine." The Lord Chief Justice explained that in <u>Eliot's case</u> (1668) 3St 331-333 (a case involving both seditious libel and the 'ordinary crime' of force used against Mr. Speaker to keep him in his chair) the House of Lords had pointed that the charge of uttering seditious words in the House was 'fully answered by the plea of Privilege' but that the charge of causing a riot in the House was not. The courts had no jurisdiction over words spoken in Parliament by a Member of Parliament, but the jurisdiction to consider criminal offences committed in the House remained'. A fortiori, the jurisdiction to consider criminal offences committed outside the House, for example, in a Member's office, also remained.

The Court of Appeal of Ontario rejected the position of the accused in *Regina v. Bernier*[71] that the Board had the "exclusive jurisdiction" concerning the proper use of moneys involved in the fraud charges and held that Parliament had not in any way manifested an intention to set aside the jurisdiction of the courts presently authorized to apply the Criminal Code. While the Board may exclusively give opinions on the proper use of members' budgetary funds, this did not have the effect of supplanting the Criminal Code nor the jurisdiction of the courts to apply the *Code* while the function of the Board to decide on the proper use of these funds. The Court of Appeal of the Province of Quebec was of the same view in *Regina v. Fontaine*.[72]

The second scenario concerns what is meant by the "official capacity" of a member of parliament. "Official capacity" is much wider than the member of Parliament's role while he is involved in a parliamentary proceeding. The functions of a member in his "official capacity" include assisting constitutents in matters attributable to his status as a member of the House of Commons. In Canada it is a crime for a member to corruptly accept money for doing something in his "official capacity". In 1964 a court found that a member of the House of Commons who agrees to accept money from a constituent for the use of his influence to bring about the purchase of the government of certain lands, is acting in his "official capacity". The member was convicted of corruption while acting in his "official capacity".[73]

The Canadian Court in the above scenario's definition of "official capacity" relied on a decision of the Judicial Committee of the Privy Council (U.K.), hearing an appeal in 1963 from Ceylon (now Sri Lanka). The Judicial Committee said that "given the proper anxiety of the House of Commons to confine its own or its members' privileges to the minimum infringement of the liberties of others, it is important to see that those privileges do not cover activities that are not squarely within a member's true function." It was considering a "statute which made it an offence to offer a bribe to a member "in his capacity as such member." The Judicial Committee expressly recognized that "the question of what are "proceedings in Parliament", when the member is protected by parliamentary immunity, though clearly related, is narrower than the functions or capacities of a member as such. Indeed it could hardly be otherwise. A member of Parliament is clearly fulfilling his functions as a member when he visits with or receives his constituents, opens fund drives, presides at local meetings, or carries out any number of other tasks, but to pass from that proposition of the statement that all these activities are "proceedings in Parliament" is a step I am not prepared to take."[74]

As this relates to criminal activity while functioning as member of Parliament, it is now therefore clear that a member's "official capacity" is broader than his function during proceedings in parliament. The courts' lesson to note here is that members of parliament in the English tradition cannot escape criminal liability <u>as parliamentarians</u> by invoking the narrower "proceedings in Parliament" concept and trying to subsume under that concept the broader "official capacity".[*] Members of parliament in the continental European tradition might adopt this lesson instead of claiming absolute inviolability for themselves in order to escape the criminal process in all circumstances, whether in or out of parliament, when engaged in their official capacity.

Parliament is the place where members who make laws should also make allegations of corruption and abuse of power by government. In so doing, they enjoy the privilege of freedom of speech and immunity, as indeed they should, for the proper

---

[*] A criminal act such as assaulting a fellow member during a proceeding in Parliament has nothing to do with the proceeding in Parliament.

functioning of parliament. But when legislators arrogate to themselves the discretion to decide whether members should face the criminal process, the situation is ripe with political overtures. The stench of political favouritism and corruption permeates the atmosphere.

Parliament should leave to the executive's prosecutorial arm the discretionary decision to lay criminal charges, and to an independent judiciary the task of adjudicating on the propriety of such charges. Modern constitutionalism, the separation of powers, and the rule of law require it. The people expect it.

Chapter 6
<u>Parliamentary inviolability in practice around the world</u>

In this chapter the reader is invited to see what happens when parliamentary inviolability rather than parliamentary immunity is in place. To those raised in the culture of parliamentary immunity in particular, it raises questions and concerns about the rule of law, equality before the law, and, good governance. For that matter, every country in the United Nations will flag the rule of law and equality before the law as part of their heritage, past or present.

The irony is that most of the constitutions of those countries spell out the traditional liberal democratic constraints on how the power of the state can be exercised, by providing for the separation of the executive, legislative, and judicial powers. Yet each of these constitutions that provides for parliamentary inviolability represents a contradiction of the separation of powers, as it allows the legislative branch to take on and meddle in the roles of the executive branch and the judicial branch in the inquisitorial systems of law.

Chapter 7 concludes this book with a final argument for the abolition of inviolability. But before such argument, the present chapter shows how in practice parliamentary inviolability works in many parts of the world. This survey of the concrete reality of inviolability intends to strengthen the reader's grasp of the need for the Chapter 7 discussion.

This chapter arranges the examples alphabetically by country for ease of reference only. My brief accompanying commentary hopes to shed light. Recall that 'inviolability' refers to immunity from criminal process.

ALBANIA

In 2004, an opposition member of Parliament in Albania who also was the editor of a newspaper wrote an article accusing the prime minister's wife of illegal activities (with her husband's support), and of spying for Greece. The opposition member's inviolability made it a problem for the wife to sue, so her husband the prime minister moved, unsuccessfully, to lift the member's parliamentary inviolability.[75] Here we see the inviolability of the opposition member allowing him to flout the rule of law, while at the same time occasioning political subterfuge.

BELGIUM

<u>Reuters</u> fait rapport le 18 novembre 1996 que la Belgique s'est enfoncée un peu dans les scandales lundi avec le dépôt d'une demande de mise en accusation du vice-Premier ministre belge Elio di Rupo, éclaboussé par les allégations de pédophille....

La Chambre devrait créer une commission spéciale qui devra décider de l'opportunité de lever son immunité parlementaire.

<u>The New York Times</u> reported 19 November 1996, Belgium's Government slid deeper into crisis today as the Parliament began investigating allegations that a Deputy Prime Minister had engaged in sex with under age boys. The investigation was the latest turn in a scandal involving abductions, sexual abuse and murder that has shaken Belgians since the police broke up a pedophile ring in August, rescuing

two kidnapped girls and discovering the bodies of two more. Since then, disclosures of police and judicial bungling, and suggestions of involvement and a cover up by high-level politicians, have shattered confidence in the Government. Today, a prliamentary commission held its first meeting to review the charges against Deputy Prime Minister Elio di Rupo, who has vigorously denied the allegations, which surfaced in the Belgian press last weekend. Mr. Di Rupo was himself in charge of Belgium's fight against porn on the internet..... The commission which could take days to reach a conclusion, must decide whether to recommend lifting Mr. Di Rupo's immunity from prosecution and sending him before Belgium's highest court. The commission consists of 11 people, seven from the ruling center-left party and four from opposition parties..... Last month, in a show of public discust with the political and judicial system, 250,000 people marched in Brussels to support the parents of murdered and missing children.

The Irish Times 18 November 1996 reported that Belgium's deputy prime minister, Elio di Rupo, accused of having sex with minors, is to face further investigation by the country's top country, the Cour de Cassation. However, his parliamentary colleagues yesterday refused, on the advice of their committee of inquiry, to take the more drastic step of removing his parliamentary immunity and laying formal charges against him. Criminal charges against ministers can only be laid by parliament, and the subsequent trial must be before the Cour de Cassation.

The Gazette (Montreal) reported December 10,1996, Belgium's Supreme Court ruled yesterday that evidence of pedophilia is not sufficient grounds to lift the parliamentary immunity of a vice-premier....Two weeks ago, parliament agreed there is not enough evidence to support the allegations, but urged prosecutors of the Supreme Court to continue the investigation.

The Guardian reported 13 December 1996, Elio di Rupo, the Belgian deputy prime minster, was cleared of having sex with under-age boys by a parliamentary committee which voted yesterday on party lines not to jeopardise the government by bringing a crimal case against him......The vote was seven to four, the coalition partners voting for

The deputy prime minister and the opposition voting against. ` This is an exclusively political decision. It is not what the public expected,' said Didier Trusgnach of the liberals. Bur a socialist deputy retorted: ' The allegations were increduly light. I didn't know whether to laugh or cry.'....Mr. di Rupo was able to survive because he retained the backing of the coalition of Socialists and Christian Democrats, and the Francophone media despite the reluctance of Mr. Dehaene to give open support.....The government promised yesterday to introduce new laws to allow allegations against politicians to be investigated by the judicial authorities without prior parliamentary approval.

BRAZIL

From Brazil, it is reported by Mark Colvin in 2009 that in a case that gives a dark new twist to reality television, a popular Barzilian crime show host has allegedly been commissioning murders to boost his ratings. Dina Rosendorff in turn reported television host Wallace Souza's reality cime series, Canal Livre, built up a huge audience in the city of Manaus. The show featured dramatic footage of police raids and arrests. Souza was often the first on the scene, approaching freshly burnt corpses and railing against rampant crime. Now Brazilian investigators say the popular presenter's knack for being first at a murder scene is more than just a coincidence. But despite being under investigation, he remains free due to a quirk in the system which gives him immunity (inviolability) because he is politician.[76]

Another report points out the same presenter of a TV crime show in Brazil is supected of ordering killings to increase his ratings with graphic footage of murder scenes. The TV host remains free because of immunity (inviolability) that prevents him being arrested as long as he is politician.[77]

CAMBODIA

In 2005, opposition leader Sam Rinsy filed a lawsuit accusing Prime Minister Hun Sen of trying to blow him up in a 1997 grenade attack that killed at least 16 people. As is common in Cambodian political feuds, the prime minister countered with a defamation suit and then took the step of having the Parliament strip Sam Rinsy and two of his colleagues of their parliamentary immunity to permit the defamation suit to proceed.[78] Thus inviolability, which is contrary to the rule of law and the principle of equality before the general law, was in turn abused to satisfy a political feud.

CAMEROON

In 2004, a member of Parliament who is also an M.P. of the ruling party was implicated along with 11 other persons who are not members. They are all awaiting trial in a murder case. Yet preliminary investigation would only begin in the member's instance when immunity is lifted. Here is a case of a country that claims to be subject to the rule of law permitting a member to be immune from the general law that implicates him and 11 others, such that he is the only person not awaiting trial. The members of the opposition party stated in a memo that it was inadmissible that, in a country said to be one where the rule of law prevails, the accused member continues to sit in the National Assembly to the consternation of the deceased's family and all Cameroonians.[79]

CENTRAL AMERICAN PARLIAMENT, PARLACAN

Parlacan came under criticism from five of the Central American presidents, particularly rejecting the abuse of the parliamentary immunity (inviolability) enjoyed by former rulers who are ex officio members of Parlacan. Parlacan President, Mario Facussé of Honduras successfully evaded prosecution on a charge of illegal land dealings thanks to his immunity (inviolability). He has since resigned. Former Nicaraguan president Arnoldo Alemán, recently convicted of corruption charges, has sought to hide behind his immunity (inviolability) as a member of Parlacan. Finally, in 2004 Honduran President César Diaz was found to be using Parlacan premises to traffic in drugs.[80] This demonstrates the havoc inviolability plays on good governance.

CHILE

When it comes to Chile, the name that appears most frequently is that of the late former president Pinochet, whose parliamentary immunity (inviolability) from prosecution for the 1974 killing of the former Chilean army chief Carlos Prats (who was living in exile in Buenos Aires), was eventually lifted in 2004. Pinochet's immunity (inviolability) had also been lifted in connection with the case involving the killings carried out in Chile as part of "Operation Condor" to eliminate political opponents.[81]

Parliamentary inviolability may play a big part in the political life of a nation, to the detriment of good governance.

In October 2004 Pia Guzmán a member of the R.N. party, (Renovacion Nacional), accused two U.D.I. senators (Union Democrata Independiente) and a senator from the ruling Concertación alliance of attending parties held by businessman

Claudio Spinak which allegedly involved the sexual exploitation of children. Her statements led to a split in the Allianza por Chile, the alliance between R.N. and U.D.I. Infuriated at Guzmán's allegations, U.D.I. brought charges of calumny against the deputy. They aimed to strip Guzmán of legislative immunity (inviolability), a prerequisite for bringing a member of Congress to trial. But the court rejected U.D.I.'s charges, taking into account the fact that Guzmán had never mentioned any names.[82]

CHINA

Where decisions come from on high, the vice governor of scandal-plagued Liaoning province was removed from his post in 2003 for taking bribes; he was also removed from his position as a delegate to the Liaoning Peoples Congress, which effectively cancelled his parliamentary immunity (inviolability) from prosecution.[83]

On the subject that China must follow its own path in building democratic policies, Prime Minister Wen said, "It was completely possible for us to build a democratic party with the rule of law under socialist conditions."[84] Yet in Chapter 1, we saw that in China it is not the rule of law that prevails, but rather the rule by law. Under rule by law, the law can serve as a mere tool for a government that suppresses the human person in a legalistic fashion.

CZECH REPUBLIC

Once again the decision to prosecute is in the hands of elected members rather than the executive branch of government, with the court playing a part. A news report notes the police suspect a Senator of corruption and request the ability to prosecute but can't undertake it unless the

Senator's immunity (inviolability) from prosecution is lifted.[85] Justice delayed is justice denied.

In the early post communist era, it was reported on February 18, 2002:

> "According to the constitution, deputies can be prosecuted only with approval of the house of parliament of which he or she is a member.

In the cases of two former top communist functionaires, Jaromir Obzina and Jozef Lenart, the courts have recently interrupted the proceedings and are investigating whether their former deputies' immunity does not protect them against prosecution."[86]

Four days later, the Wall Street Journal reported: "The court has delayed the trial of the indicted former interior minister Jaromir Obzina while it decides whether he qualifies for parliamentary immunity (inviolability)."[87]

In another case, both the Czech justice ministry and the Prague City Court have asked the European Parliament to release a Czech member of the European Parliament for prosecution on criminal charges. The news item also noted that "in the five year election term, the EP received 16 requests from national courts for stripping MEPs of immunity (inviolability). It has met three requests and rejected 13."[88]

Finally, in another news, from Prague, "They're Europe's 'untouchables...'. Czech legislators who enjoy parliamentary immunity (inviolability) that can shield them from prosecution even long after they've left public office." Efforts by law makers to trim the protection for members have failed. "If the Parliament refuses (to lift the member's immunity so that he or she can be prosecuted), the case can never be reopened, not only during the lawmaker's term of office, but for the rest of his or her life." The following excerpt is from Associated Press article, entitled "Czech Legislators Lead Europe in Immunity Protection for Wrongdoing":

> Czech immunity includes misdemeanors committed by parliamentarians. If lawmakers commit a minor offense, such as a traffic accident that does not involve injury or death, they can decide whether to allow police to fine them or turn the case over to parliament's Mandate and Immunity Committee.
>
> In 1998, then-Czech senator Jan Kavan was driving a car that slammed into three other vehicles in Prague; nobody was injured. Citing immunity, he refused to take an alcohol test. Kavan went on to serve as foreign minister and U.N. General Assembly president 2002-03.
>
> Even the immunity committee's head, Eva Dundackova, contends the protections are outdated. "That form of immunity is a useless leftover and should be abandoned," she said.
>
> The government says it has no immediate plans to try again to modify the protections after parliament's last attempt on December 15 failed. But ordinary citizens who must answer to the authorities for their misdeeds are rankled by the protections their elected officials enjoy, and they insist the time has come to even the playing field.
>
> "Their immunity (inviolability) is outrageous," said Katerina Benova, a 32-year-old potter from Prague. "They should serve the nation – but it seems they just serve themselves".[89]

ECUADOR

Politics again plays its part in the inviolability form of immunity. Here one may add a family feud, and wonder at the independence of the judiciary in an unsettled state. In Ecuador both the judicial and the legislative branches, instead of the executive branch, are exercising prosecutorial discretion. The Latin News Daily reported

On 9 February 2004 Leon Febres Cordero, former president and leader of the opposition Partido Social Cristinao (PSC), declared himself in contempt of the pro-governmental majority's attempts to strip him of parliamentary immunity. The government's hounding of Febres Cordero does little to rid President Gutiérrez of the "dictatorial" epithet he has acquired since replacing 27 of the supreme court's 31 judges in December 2004. Considering the country's current state of agitation, with a steady increase in political violence; regular, and significant, anti-government demonstrations; and widespread international condemnation of the executive's steady accumulation of power, government zealots might profit from listening to Ximena Bohórquez, the country's first lady, who has warned congress not to stoop to "personal revenge or public vendetta". After all, Bohórquez, Gutiérrez's estranged wife and deputy for Sociedad Patriótica, was the architect of the pro-government majority block that has fortified the administration. Proceedings against Febres Cordero started on February 5 when Congress began debating whether to lift the PSC leader's parliamentary immunity (inviolability) for alleged slander of a former party colleague, Luis Almeida. Febres Cordero accused Almeida of links with Carlos Hidalgo, a well-known drug-trafficker. Congress now has 30 days to reach a decision; if it fails to do so, judgment passes to the supreme court, which, stacked in favour of the pro-government majority, is likely to decide that prosecution of Febres Cordero can go ahead.[90]

EGYPT

The abuse of parliamentary inviolability is evident in a 2005 report of the Washington Post from Egypt. Whereas it was invented to provide relief from "la puissance des baïonnettes," parliamentary inviolability was swept aside to permit the prosecution of an opposition member on a trumped-up charge.

> Last month former secretary of state Madeleine K. Albright visited Egypt on a fact-finding mission for the Council on Foreign Relations. While there, she met with officials and civil society leaders, including an opposition member of Egypt's parliament, Ayman Nour, who heads a new political party called El Ghad, or Tomorrow. In his assessment of the situation in Egypt, Nour was sharply critical of President Hosni Mubarak's failing policies. Shortly afterward -- as soon as Albright and company had left -- the parliament met in emergency session to approve a government-sponsored motion stripping Nour of his parliamentary immunity. Minutes later, as he was leaving the parliament building, he was arrested by members of the notorious State Security Agency. His home and party headquarters were raided and searched, and computers and many of his papers were seized.

> In the days that followed, the state-controlled media competed in denouncing Nour, calling him a crook and accusing him of forgery and of lying about the membership of his party. The state security prosecutor ordered him held in solitary confinement for 45 days.[91]

EUROPEAN PARLIAMENT

The rule of law tradition congealed into existence in England in a slow, unplanned manner that commenced in the Middle Ages with no simple source or starting point. Thus since the inception of Parliament in the thirteenth century a member of the U.K. Parliament has been completely without any immunity if he was criminally charged; and since 1770, a member has been without any immunity if he was pursued in a civil action for events that did not occur during a proceeding in Parliament. Accordingly, in 2004 a U.K. member of the European Parliament who is being so pursued in a civil action, is open to the provisions of Article 10(a) of the Protocol because he is subject to the lack of parliamentary immunity (inviolability) in effect in the U.K.[92]

In 2003, Guiseppe Gargani, an Italian Member of the European Parliament (MEP) made a request to the EP for immunity as he was being sued for publishing a reply to an article written by the Public Prosecutor that reflected on the initiatives put forward by Mr. Gargani's political party. The EP said that by writing and publishing his reply, Mr. Gargani was exercising his freedom of speech in connection with the performance of his duties as a Mep and that the EP consistently taken it as a fundamental principle that immunity may on no account be waived in cases in which the acts of which a Member stands accused were carried out in the performance of his or her political duties or were directly related to those duties. (Report 2003/2183 Imm)

Note that Mr. Gargani was at no material time involved in a proceeding of the EP but rather beyond its walls, the rule of law requires that they be like everybody else. Mr. Gargani was elected to and may have replied during a proceeding in parliament with impunity.

FRANCE

In the Sénate, between 1958 and 1994 there were eleven requests to lift the inviolability of a member, nine initiated by the Ministère public, two on the initiative of civil parties. Six were accepted. Since 1995, five requests have been made and three accepted (two were accommodated in part). With respect to requests for the suspension of prosecution or detention, all nine of the requests made since 1958 were accepted.

Patrick Fraisseix goes on to describe the system thus:

> Tout au plus certaines "affaires" impliquant des personnalités marquantes du monde parlementaire (et des affaires) ont-elles attiré l'attention collective en raison du caractère extrêmement médiatique de leur déroulement et des acteurs visés, et donné le sentiment exagéré de pancacre politiquo-médiatiquo-judiciaire pour lequel la Ve République et le Parlement n'étaient que peu préparés. L'on constate en revanche une protection certaine entreprise par les Chambres au profit de leurs membres en ce sens que les autorisations de levée des immunités parlementaires demeurent quantitativement rares par rapport aux demandes formulées, alors que parallèlement les demandes de suspension des poursuites sont souvent acceptées. Joseph Barthélemy et Paul Duez avaient en leur temps déjà souligné ce phénomène en constatant que «les Assemblées politiques, sont et général, extrêmement chatouilleuses lorsque leurs prérogatives ou celles de leurs membres sont en jeu. Si l'on ajoute les inévitables considérations de camaraderie, on peut dire que quand est posée la question de l'élargissement des collègues, l'Assemblée a une tendance naturelle à le résoudre par l'affirmative, toutes les fois qu'il ne s'agit pas d'un délit déshonorant, d'un délit de cupidité». Au surplus, les Républiques antérieures connurent aussi des requêtes judiciaires à l'encontre des élus nationaux nonobstant le «parlementarisme absolu» de l'époque selon la formule de Raymond Carré de Malberg. Sous la IIIe République, la Chambre des députées se prononça onze fois sur des demandes de suspensions de poursuites et les accepta à dix reprises; sous la IVe République, la même Assemblée fur saisie à trois reprises de telles demandes et accepta à chaque fois. Le Sénat, puis le Conseil de la République, ne furent quant à eux jamais saisis de ces demandes sous les IIIe et IVe Républiques.[93]

GEORGIA

In Georgia, a member of the dominant force in Parliament was arrested in 2004 for exacting bribes from a businessman. The member had helped the new president get to power. A vote in Parliament was scheduled to lift the member's parliamentary immunity (inviolability).[94] Such a "dilemma" for the new president would not be in the cards where the rule of law prevails along with independent prosecutorial discretion.

GUATEMALA

Two branches of government, the courts and Parliament, are here both involved in prosecutorial discretion. It was reported in 2003 that "Guatemala's Supreme Court has rejected a request for the lifting of the parliamentary immunity of the leader of congress, a former dictator accused of abuse of authority and misuse of public funds, local media reported ... The request to remove the protection from prosecution was directed at the head of national Congress, Jose Efrain Rios Montt, and ruling party lawmaker Aristides Crespo. The court rejected the request on the grounds of "lack of evidence", according to the reports. Retired Gen. Otto Perez, chairman of the Patriot Party, requested in January that Rios Montt and Crespo, who also heads the ruling Guatemalan Republican Front (FRG) party's legislative block, be stripped of their parliamentary immunity. Perez accused the pair of abuse of authority, dereliction of duty and misappropriation of government funds to finance a mass rally that took place in capital's main square on Jan. 14."[95]

From Guatemala, it was reported in 2004 former President Alfonso Portillo left Guatemala shortly after the constitutional court stripped him and his former Vice-President, Francisco Reyes, of parliamentary inviolability from prosecution, which they enjoyed ex-officio as members of the Central

American parliament, Parlacen. Whether flight, as claimed in the Guatemalan press, or a previously arranged trip, he beat by hours an injunction sought by chief prosecutor Carlos de Leon. Portillo and Reyes are charged with money laundering and misuse of public funds. The immunity shield was lifted as the result of a private lawsuit seeking a ruling that the treaty creating Parlacen in 1991 was unconstitutional.[96]

GUINEA BISSAU

In 2004 in Guinea Bissau, members of the former government who remained in Parliament (and were protected by parliamentary immunity (inviolability)), were pursued by the Attorney General on charges of "large scale fraud." The Attorney General asked the Speaker to have their protection waived.[97] Politics again plays its part in the use/abuse of parliamentary inviolability.

ISRAEL

In that hot-bed of politics since its establishment, Israel, in 2001 the Knesset lifted the parliamentary inviolability of the only M.P. for the Balad Party "from pending prosecution of the criminal charges for making anti-Israel comments and organizing visits to Syria.[98] Around 30 deputies have lost their immunity (inviolability) in the past for corruption and abuse of power but a vote backing the panel's decision would be the first time it has happened for mere words". The prosecutorial discretion excercised by the legislative branch rather than the executive branch alone provides an additional occasion to raise the issue of parliamentary inviolability.

Two years later, in 2003, Letters to the Editor of the Jerusalem Post noted that a "farcical" rule for Members of Knesset rears its head in the failed attempt to lift an M.P.'s parliamentary immunity (inviolability). "The problem is that the law regarding such immunity in Israel is totally without merit compared to the U.S.'s. There has never been immunity for acts committed outside or unrelated to members' immediate legislation duties. In all such areas, members have no authority over other citizens."

The letter continues,

> There is no need for Knesset committees to decide whether MK's should or should not have their parliamentary immunity lifted. Had the Knesset enough courage to adopt a Basic Law similar to the time-honored U.S. constitutional provision, it would go a long way toward reforming MK's judicial conduct as well as marking the beginning of badly-needed judicial reform.[99]

The following is an excerpt from another letter of the same day,

> Minister of Justice Yosef Lapid took the words right out of my mind: "Lapid accused those who voted in favor of maintaining Blumenthal's immunity of thinking only of their own best interest. He said they wanted to continue the precedent of immunity in these situations in case they should be similarly charged."

> There are still unsolved cases against secular and religious politicians that should have been resolved prior to elections. How can anyone have confidence in Israel justice when politicians are thus protected?[100]

Subsequently, on May 18, 2003 an editorial in the Jerusalem Post questioned the role of the Knesset in waiving or defending the parliamentary immunity (inviolability) of a member of the Knesset (MK). The Knesset had refused to lift the member's immunity and a third party petitioned the High Court of

Justice to rule against the decision of the Knesset to retain the member's parliamentary immunity (inviolability).

The editorial goes on:

> Members are not entitled to place their person above the law. Their only concern is making sure that the request of lifting an MK's immunity is free from any hint of political prosecution, discrimination, or departure from accepted prosecution norms. The editorial said a number of MK's accused the prosecution of hounding small fry like Blumenthal, while dragging their feet for years on the matter of Ehud Barak's unprecedented network of bogus N.P.O.s, which according to the state comptroller, were nothing but fronts for funneling illicit funds to his campaign coffers... no MK should appear to enjoy privileges denied ordinary folk...
>
> There is an increasingly disturbing sense among politicians that the judicial system is out to get them. Thus, if the High Court does reverse the committee's decision, this too will add grist to the mill of politicians' distrustful of the courts. The very existence of such suspicions makes it all the more urgent that a thorough review be undertaken of whether politicians can be relied upon to fairly judge their peers. If MK's abuse our trusting them to impartially distinguish between political harassment and legitimate law enforcement, then perhaps it is time to carefully consider a more dependable mechanism for establishing when our parliamentary representatives deserve immunity from prosecution.[101]

While the editorial ends by saying that the MK's cannot afford to forget that justice must not only be done, but must be seen to be done, there is no mention of the separation of powers in a liberal democracy such as Israel. Such separation, dictates that it is the executive branch that is entrusted with the independent prosecutorial discretion to distinguish between political harassment and legitimate law enforcement, and, it is the responsibility of the independent judiciary to render justice transparently.

ITALY

The reader has noted earlier (see frontis piece) that in April 1993, the Craxi affair saw "the cabinet office issued a statement saying the Craxi affair made it essential to change the voting system quickly, and political sources said Ciampi (Prime Minister) also planned to scrap parliamentary immunity from prosecution....After hearing Mr. Craxi's counsel warn them of a witch hunt and tell them, "Tomorrow it will be your turn", the members of the Chamber of Deputies voted narrowly to allow the former Socialist leader to keep his parliamentary immunity on all but a few minor charges."[102]

In October 1993, Article 68 of the Constitution was amended to remove the immunity (inviolability) of MPs from being criminally prosecuted, while focusing the immunity (inviolability) on the prevention of imprisonment, detention or any limitation of the freedom of a member of the Chamber of Deputies. The limitation was made following several cases in which members abused the immunity (inviolability) provided to them. In the years 1992-93 more than 200 requests were made to lift immunity (inviolability). Cases are known in which the refusal of the house to lift the inviolability enabled members to escape the country. It is for this reason that the content of the immunity (inviolability) was changed.[*]

The issue of parliamentary immunity continued to ferment because Italy "is a country in which political partisanship has long permeated almost every public institution."[103]

---

[*] Background Document on: Parliamentary Immunity- Members of Parliament Inviolability Comparative view, May 19, 2003, the Knesset Research and Information Center.

In July 2002, a member of Silvio Berlusconi's Forza Italia party presented a bill to grant M.P.s immunity from criminal prosecution (inviolability) while they sit in Parliament. If the measure becomes law, criminal investigations into or trials against members of parliament, Constitutional court judges or Italy's president will be frozen until the person concerned has finshed their term of office. The opposition said "it's a scandal because it introduces a regime of absolute privilege for M.P.s with respect to normal citizens [...] some form of parliamentary immunity was normal [...], you cannot extend immunity of this type to impunity: [...] its a slap in the face to citizens." The measure was said to be "aimed at getting Premier Berlusconi and some of his associates out of their ongoing legal troubles."[104]

In January 2003, the secretary of the judges and prosecutors union said of the proposal that "M.P.s must be subject to the law like any other citizen... It's inconceivable that those who make the laws, should not be subject to them". Tensions between the judiciary and the centre-right have been steadily mounting since Berlusconi came to power in May 2001... Members of the judiciary, supported by the opposition, say the reforms are designed to undermine the judiciary's independence and autonomy, as well as prevent them from investigating corruption allegations involving politicians..."[105] The government has defended the overhaul by saying it only wants to bring the Italian system into line with the European countries, most of which have systems where the executive exerts influence over the work of prosecutors.

Apart from restoring immunity to M.P.s from criminal prosecution, the bill would "discipline magistrates who have become too involved in politics." The justice minister said, "It is the only way to achieve a turning point in the relationship between politicians and magistrates....In civilized countries, judges cannot try those who govern."[106]

In June 2003, a bill which gives the prime minister and others, the speakers of the two houses and head of the constitutional court, immunity (inviolability) from prosecution was passed. It provoked an opposition Senator to say, "It is not a scandal to discuss parliamentary immunity ... what is scandalous is to think that immunity becomes impunity – people (getting) elected not to serve their country but to avoid being prosecuted."[107]

The Constitutional Court in January 2004 declared the June 18 2003 law illegitimate, saying it violated the constitutionally enshrined principle that all citizens are equal before the law. But government hawks blasted the ruling as "political."[108]

The June 18 2003 law granting parliamentary immunity (inviolability) was rushed through Parliament in record time in order to save the premier Berlusconi the embarrassment of a possible conviction during Italy's six-month stint as European Union duty president, which ended in December 2003. The Democratic Left leader said of the ruling of the Constitutional Court that the "rule of law has triumphed." The leader of the Green Party said, "This is an important day for democracy in the country... Despite the centre-right's attacks on the basic principles of democracy, the Constitution's system of checks and balances held up..."[109]

Interestingly, Sandro Bouli, the national coordinator of Forza Italia, said that the decision of the Constitutional Court denying the bill and thus the provision of immunity from criminal prosecution to the prime minister and the Speaker of the two houses, "was modeled on norms existing in other European countries. We can now consider ourselves less European."[110]

Earlier we noted that in liberal democratic societies at least, constitutions impose broad conditions – or constraints

– on how the power of a state can be exercised. They include: the idea of separation of powers and absolute limits on what the state or its officials may do.

A modern constitution governs not the people but the government itself. It should provide the essential framework for orderly government, its inter-relation and its limits. Of signal importance is the role of the judiciary, whose duty is to uphold the constitution, to be its protector and guarantor. Because the judiciary is the guardian of the constitution and the laws enacted under it, Italy is considered to be a liberal democratic society.

In October 2009, the June 18, 2003 law which shields the Prime Minister (Berlusconi), the speakers of the two houses and the head of the constitutional court, was ruled unconstitutional by Italy's Constitutional court, as it breached the Article of the Constitution making all citizens equal before the law. One of Mr. Berlusconi's lawyers had argued that he is no longer 'first among equals', but ought to be considered 'First above equals'.[111]

LATVIA

In 2004 in Latvia, Parliament was required to lift the inviolability of members to prosecute three left-wing (pro-Russia) members for organizing unauthorized protest events "against education reform."[112] Once again the final prosecutorial discretion was taken out of the hands of the independent prosecutor and the rule of law was watered down.

MACEDONIA

In April 2004, in Macedonia, a parliamentary committee lifted the parliamentary immunity (inviolability) of a member who was a former interior minister and head of the police, at the request of an investigative judge. It was revealed that the killings of seven alleged Pakistanian terrorists two years earlier were staged to win U.S. support and that the victims were innocent illegal immigrants.[113]

Serious criminal offences and national security concern the public interest. The criminal law applies to protect the public interest. Prosecution of criminals and terrorists is a matter for the executive branch of government, not the legislative branch, which is the venue for debate on those issues. The criminal law applies to protect the public interest of state security and trumps the legislative branch and its need for members to attend regular parliamentary sittings.

MEXICO

When threatened in 2003 with their immunity (inviolability) being waived by the government party in Parliament, members who were also oil-union officials of the former government successfully used the procedure available to request the judiciary to suspend the proceedings to lift their immunity (inviolability) and thus to shield them from charges of embezzlement and abuse of power.[114] Thus the judiciary is involved in prosecutorial discretion, which in a liberal democracy properly belongs to the executive branch of government.

In 2005, the threat to strip a potential candidate of his parliamentary immunity and to prosecute occasioned the press to print that "during the PRI (Institutional Revolutionary Party) years, the judiciary was under the effective control of the executive branch of government."[115]

The abolition of parliamentary inviolability is more viable where there is an authoritative rule of law in a nation that has a political morality.

The "corruption video saga" in 2004 saw the Parliament lift the parliamentary immunity (inviolability) of René Bejarano, a deputy of the PRD (Partido de la Revolucion Democratica) who was Mexico City Mayor Lopez C. Brador's private secretary. 'He was taped stuffing dollars into his pockets, that appeared to have come from a dodgy property developer, Carlos Ahumada.'

> Bejarano says, that Ahumada, facing severe financial difficulties, conspired with Salinas (former president of Mexico) and Robles (former president of PRD) to topple Mexico City mayor Andrés López Obrador.[116]

MOLDOVA

Politics once again has a hand in the use of parliamentary inviolability. From Moldova we read of the ruling Communist Party in the Parliament in February 2004 stripping the leader of the Muslim party of his immunity (inviolability) in a vote in which the opposition party did not take part, saying they did not want "to take part in the communists' political game." The week before, three other opposition members suffered the same fate. In all of those cases, the prosecutor had requested Parliament to strip them of their immunity for organizing unsanctioned protest rallies and for defaming the national symbols of other countries. They were accused of setting ablaze a Russian flag and a portrait of then Russian president Vladimir Putin during a protest rally in November 2003.[117] (This activity may have been permitted under Protocol 10 of the European Parliament if Moldova had been a member. Protocol 10 expects members to be immune when involved in political rallies.)

MONTENEGRO

In Montenegro it appears the Assembly not only withdraws the immunity of its deputies but also may lift the same immunity that is enjoyed by judges. In 2004, a court requested the stripping of parliamentary immunity (inviolability) of two deputies. In addition, according to a report, the Assembly also lifted the judicial immunity of a judge so that criminal proceedings could be set in motion. The chairman of the relevant committee said this was done so that the prosecution could take place to enable the deputy to prove his innocence.[118]

All this permits a further conflict for the legislative branch to be involved in the prosecutorial discretion of not only its own members but of members of the judicial branch, which is expected to be independent and separate from the legislative branch and the executive branch.

NICARAGUA

In 2001 a former Nicaraguan president was continuing to enjoy parliamentary inviolability from the sexual abuse charges based on allegations by his step-daughter which he denied because fellow legislators refused to lift his immunity.[119]

The decision to prosecute criminal offences rests with the executive branch. This also avoids an appearance of bias where there is a balanced constitution.

POLAND

After Parliament had stripped them of their parliamentary immunity (inviolability) in 2003, three former deputies of the Parliament in Poland (including a former minister) were convicted in 2005 for leaking police information to organized crime groups about an impending police raid and for endangering undercover policemen.[120]

Serious criminal offences concern the public interest and the criminal law applies to protect the public interest of state security. Parliamentarians should have no role in prosecutorial discretion. Law-makers should be subject to the laws they pass.

PORTUGAL

In a liberal democracy, the executive (police/prosecutors) decides who and when to prosecute. In Portugal the constitution provides that the judiciary and the Parliament each have a role in prosecutorial discretion. A probe into an alleged child sex ring involved a member of Parliament. The member asked and received of Parliament a release from his parliamentary immunity (inviolability) in 2003 in order to be heard by the police. After questioning, a criminal court in May ordered that he be held in preventative detention. Parliament's ethics committee then voted to allow the member to resume his mandate as an M.P. In October an appeal court ordered the member to be released under police protection because the preventative detention was not justified.[121] On December 31, 2003, ten persons including the member were charged with crimes involving children.[122]

Parliamentarians in a liberal democracy should have no input into the exercise of prosecutorial discretion, nor should the developed rules governing the circumstances concerning when a person may be released on bail be altered at their behest.

RUSSIAN FEDERATION

Parliamentary inviolability is often a vehicle for bad elements in society to escape the law. In effect, members of the State

Duma, the lowest house of the Russian Parliament, decide who will be prosecuted because of the fact that "tomorrow it will be your turn". Reports in the press regarding the Duma and its members have, since 1995, shown that while the spirit to change or abolish parliamentary immunity (inviolability) may from time to time be willing, the flesh is weak*. Moves in the Duma to abolish parliamentary inviolability have rarely succeeded. These reports also show that the Duma and the Prosecution Service combine to determine whether a member may be arrested, prosecuted, detained or searched. Such a combination is anathema to good governance for it combines two constitutional powers. In liberal democratic societies, legislative authority and executive authority are separated.

In 1995, it was reported by Geoffrey York there is a danger that the next Duma "may become a congress of thieves", said Stanislav Govorushkin, leader of a nationalist faction in the Duma. It is facing a flood of new candidates with criminal records who are scrambling to get elected so they can enjoy immunity from prosecution. The State Duma, [...] trying to launch crackdown on the worst offenders in its midst, voted to lift the parliamentary immunity of a member. The member in question was accused of bilking Russians of an estimated $1 billion in a pyramid investment scheme and admitted that he sought election in order to gain parliamentary immunity (inviolability). At all levels of government, in almost 160 cases, prosecutors had enough evidence to file charges against elected officials but the politicians were protected by their parliamentary immunity (inviolability), according to Oleg Gaidanov, the deputy prosecutor general. In one case, he said, investigators had concluded that a deputy had "killed

---

* Russia, 20 Jan. 2000, Ros Business Consulting; Moscow, 19 Sept. 2000, BBC, text of report by Russian Laws Agency Ekho Moskvy (poll of Muscovites show 93% favour abolition); 20 Sept. 2000, Reuters; Russia 20 Sept. 2000, Ros Business Consulting; Moscow, 10 Nov. 2004, Interfax Laws Services.

people in cold blood" and should be charged with murder and illegal possession of weapons. But the Duma refused to lift the deputy's immunity, and the case had to be dropped.[123]

In 1998, it was again reported that "a growing number of Russian criminals were seeking elected office to gain immunity from prosecution. In an election in Nobember 1998 in the Krasnodar region, a police official said 10 candidates had criminal records and 28 more were suspected of having criminal connections."[124]

In 1999, it was reported that "immunity from prosecution is perhaps the biggest perk of a seat in the State Duma, the lowest house of Russian Parliament. If a criminal can win election to the Duma, it is virtually impossible for the police to pursue charges against him. [...] Among the candidates on the election ballots in December 1999 will be dozens of gangsters, prisoners, convicted or suspected criminals, corrupt businessmen, and other shadowy characters who all under police investigation. [...] Candidates included Boris Berezovsky, the wealthy tycoon who is under police investigation on suspicion of stealing millions of dollars from Aeroflot, and four candidates who are reportedly wanted by police on extortion and other charges. Analoty Bykov, an aluminum industry mogul who fled to Hungary when he was charged with gun-running and complicity in two gangland-style killings, was given the no. 2 position on the candidate list of Vladimir Zhirinovsky's ultra-nationalist party, until the electoral commission disallowed it."[125]

On the other hand there remains concern in Russia for "la puissance des baïonnettes". "I can speak out strongly today against the West, Clinton, Zionism and the fifth column in Russia and in the Duma, Communist member Vasily Shandybin told the chamber. If our immunity is removed, tomorrow they can arrest Vasily Ivanovich Shandybin and the newspapers will say what a bad guy he was." Oleg Finko of the nationalist Liberal Democratic Party said deputies had nothing to fear as long as "refined, peace-loving Vladimir Vladimirovich Putin" remained as president. But suppose a new Nicholas II came to power tomorrow? he said, referring to Russia's last czar. "We don't know which groups of deputies would have to go into exile…"[126]

A bill, which was defeated in September 2000, proposed by the reformist Union of Right Forces, would have allowed prosecutors to open criminal cases against Duma deputies without securing the chamber's approval. But detentions, arrests, and searches of Duma lawmakers would still need to be authorized by the house, the Interfax news agency reported. Communists and ultra-nationalists spoke harshly of the proposed bill, claiming that limiting legislative immunity would allow the government to persecute lawmakers for opposition-minded speeches.[127]

In the case of deputy Vladimir Gulovlyov (V.G.), prosecutors in 2001 accused this former long-serving (ten years) deputy governor of the Chlyabinsk region in the Urals with "illegal financial activity" or fraud. When the prosecutor demanded that the Duma lift his immunity, senior Duma members wanted to lead more detailed allegations against V.G. before voting.[128]

In the interim, in July 2001, then president Putin signed a controversial law drastically limiting the number of political parties, and providing state financing to the surviving few – a measure heavily criticized by liberals. Putin argued that the law would keep corrupt businessmen from funding fly-by-night parties to buy themselves the immunity from prosecution that goes with a parliamentary seat.[129]

The move to strip deputy V.G. of his immunity did not succeed. While most members of the Commission of the

Duma supported a request by the prosecutor general to do so, far from all agreed to his arrest and a search of his home. For instance… "seven members of the Commission were only for stripping V.G. of his deputy's status, five did not object to his arrest and a search, one rejected all measures, while another one abstained."[130]

Deputy V.G. was ultimately stripped of his parliamentary immunity. He became the third parliamentarian to lose his immunity (inviolability) 'in the eight year history of a lower house famed for fiercely defending the privileged, above – the – law status of its lower house. V.G. launched a judicial appeal against the Duma's decision, saying the accusations were politically based and stemmed from his opposition to the Kremlin.[131] While the prosecutor was given consent by the Duma to prosecute him and search his house, the Duma refused to allow the prosecutor-general's office to arrest him. The saga of Deputy V.G. ended in August 2001. He was killed when unknown attackers shot him and escaped.[132]

The combination of the prosecutor general and three Supreme Court judges is required for the prosecutor general to issue criminal charges against a member of Parliament. But then the prosecutor general must send an inquiry to the Duma requesting the revocation of immunity. Accordingly Moscow based lawyer Dimitri Agranovski explained to Nezavisimaya Gazeta, Vladimir Zhirinovsky need not fear because the Duma will never consent to Vladimir Zhirinovsky being prosecuted.[133]

A change in the political culture of the Duma was noticed in 2004 when deputy Shashurin, a businessman and three-time convict (hooliganism and embezzlement) was arrested by officials of the Tatarstan Interior Ministry, accused of embezzling $105,000 (US) from a commercial firm. His parliamentary immunity had been lifted three months earlier. The report goes on under the heading "Significance":

> The Shashurin type of parliamentary deputy is on the decline in Russia. Many shady businessmen had previously sought immunity from prosecution by becoming parliamentary deputies. He may also have fallen foul of hardline Tatar President Mintmin Shamiyev, whom he ran against for presidency of the republic in 2001. Parliamentary deputies now are more likely to be businessmen seeking to lobby for their interests or technocratic party activists.[134]

In 2004, the debate on a bill before the Russian Duma to restrict parliamentary immunity (inviolability) (that had been introduced in 2001) that did not pass, noted that <u>Art 98</u> of the Constitution guarantees parliamentary immunity (inviolability) from prosecutorial enforcement measures like arrest, detention or search, but the sponsor of the bill said that initiating a criminal case, conducting an investigation, and also carrying out judicial proceedings involving a deed committed by a parliamentarian does not need to be authorized by a lawmaking body.[135] Perhaps without realizing it the sponsor was bringing home the liberal democratic notion that the legislative branch of the government should not be involved in prosecutorial discretion, that role belongs to the executive branch.

In February 20, 2007 the Globe and Mail reports that "Russia's top court has ruled there's enough evidence to lift the parliamentary immunity of a politician accused of fraudulently taking over a Canadian-operated luxury hotel. (Halifax based IMP Group International Inc.) The country's Supreme Court made the rare ruling in a verbal decision Feb. 9, a spokesman for the high court confirmed yesterday. Unless an appeal is launched, the case against Rifat Shaikhutdinov will be sent to the Duma, the Russian Parliament, for a vote on whether he can be prosecuted....Several experts on Russian politics say the Duma will likely approve a criminal prosecution. Tom Remington, a professor at Emory University in Atlanta, G.A., said Mr. Shaikhutdinov's party has seen its power wane in recent years, while Russian President Vladimir Putin's United Russia party dominates." All Putin has to do is say, "Yes, sacrifice this individual, and he will be sacrificed." Prof. Remington also noted that Russia is preparing for a general election later this year, and Mr. Putin's party has pledged to stamp out corruption. Vladimir Gladyshev, a Moscow lawyer and Duma observer, said that if the matter comes to a vote, "it means the whole thing has been agreed to at the very top." However, he added, some deputies can be expected to resist the lifting of immunity "on principle." The lifting of criminal immunity for federal politicians is rare in Russia, having happened only four times in recent memory."[*]

SAO TOME

Changes in government, along with the government's use of its majority to waive parliamentary inviolability produced political games in Sao Tome in 2005. Two opposition members wanted to rescind their parliamentary immunity so that they could face questioning by a tribunal investigating the embezzlement of aid funds.

It was reported that:

> Basilio Diogo, the secretary-general of the Movement of Democratic Forces for Change (MDFM), has joined with Arzemiro dos Prazeres of the Party for Democratic Convergence (PCD) in demanding that the National Assembly rescind their parliamentary inviolability so that they can face questioning by a tribunal investigating the embezzlement of aid

---

[*] The Globe and Mail, February 20, 2007. For an update on the Kremlin entitled Why Kremlin v Khodorkovsky still matters, see Amy Knight, Globe and Mail, February 9, 2007.

monies. Last October, the National Assembly had indicated its willingness to co-operate with the ministry of justice investigation, but later ruled that it would not revoke the immunity of the five MPs suspected of involvement, including former Prime Minister Maria das Neves, who was sacked last September over the scandal.[...]

Both Diogo and dos Prazeres have declared their innocence and have distanced themselves from the Assembly's ruling, anxious to demonstrate that no-one should be above the law.

Significance: The two MPs' demands will increase the pressure on the National Assembly to accede to the justice ministry's request. However, parliament may yet block the enquiry, probably on political grounds. The ruling Liberation Movement of Sao Tome and Principe (MLSTP), which holds the most seats in parliament, appears keen to protect its former Prime Minister das Neves, possibly to avoid further scrunity of other MLSTP ministers but also to prevent too much bad publicity ahead of next year's legislative election.[136]

SLOVAKIA

The Parliament in Slovakia voted at a closed meeting in June 2001 against stripping Gustav Krajci an opposition member of his parliamentary immunity (inviolability), thus rejecting a request from the investigator dealing with accusations of abuse of public office (taking a bribe) Krajci had earlier been interior minister under former premier Vladimir Meclar and had faced charges which were stopped by the court, citing an amnesty which Meclar announced when he was acting president after the former president's term had expired in March of 1998.[137]

In May 2003, the Parliament lifted the parliamentary immunity (inviolability) of a member of the opposition to permit him to be prosecuted for fraud and abuse of information. In fact the Slovak parliament has stripped several members of their immunity so that they could face prosecution.[138]

Once again the legislative branch trumps the executive branch in an activity that belongs to the executive branch; serious criminal offences concern public safety and the criminal law is applied to protect the public interest of state security.

In November 2003, the Slovak Parliament voted to lift the immunity of a member who was caught in the act of taking a bribe, although they opposed him being taken into custody. The article went on to note: "Significance, if convicted, the member faces up to eight years prison. This contrasts sharply with the failure of the Latvian parliament to strip their speaker of immunity last week for corrupt party financing..."[139]

What belongs to independent prosecutorial discretion, whether to prosecute, to take into custody, to permit bail, etc is simply not there when the legislature invokes parliamentary inviolability.

In January 2005 the Slovak Parliament lifted the parliamentary immunity (inviolability) of a member at the requested of the prosecutor general enabling her to face criminal prosecution in the case of large-scale fuel tampering.[140]

The constitution in a liberal democracy should state that the executive branch does the prosecution. Its legislative branch legislates in the area of criminal prosecution.

SLOVENIA

A report by Slovene television provided

The parliamentary Commission for Mandates and Elections unanimously approved the request of the Kranj prosecution service that parliamentary immunity (inviolability) should not be recognized to SDS (main ruling coalition Slovene

Democratic Party) MP (and Trzic Mayor) Pavle Rupar and that a criminal investigation against him to be approved. The commission proposed that the National Assembly decide on this at an open session.[141]

TOGO

A report from UFC on April 4, 2009 points that

> Le Bureau de l'Assemblée nationale du Togo a annoncé ce jeudi, avoir été saisi d'une lettre par le procureur de la République demandant la levée de l'immunité parlementaire du député Kpatcha Gnassingbé, accusé de complot et d'atteinte à la sûreté de l'État. Dans une déclaration rendue publique après une réunion convoquée d'urgence, le Bureau du Parlement togolais signale que "le procureur de la République a porté à la connaissance du président de l'Assemblée nationale des faits auxquels s'ajoutent des déclarations qui constitueraient, selon lui, un crime flagrant justifiant l'application de l'article 53 alinéa 3 de la Constitution de notre pays".

> Les déboires de ce député du Rassemblement du peuple togolais (RPT, parti au pouvoir) ont commencé dans la nuit de dimanche à lundi quand des échanges de tirs ont eu lieu entre sa garde rapprochée et des forces de sécurité publique, qui selon les autorités togolaises, étaient envoyées chez lui pour interpeller des personnes soupçonnées dans une affaires d'atteinte à la sûreté de l'État.

> Député de la préfecture de la Kozah (Nord du pays), fief du parti au pouvoir, Kpatcha Gnassingbé entretien des relations conflictuelles avec son frère président, Faure Gnassingbé, depuis son éviction du gouvernement en tant que ministre de la Défense au lendemain des législatives 2007.

> Son arrestation pour de nombreux observateurs augure des divisions au sein du parti au pouvoir

et de l'armée togolaise où il a de nombreux sympathisants.[142]

TURKEY

In a liberal democratic society, the executive branch prosecutes, the legislature legislates on crime, and the independent judiciary oversees the prosecution. Proposals in 1997 by the executive branch of the new government of Turkey to the Parliament to lift the parliamentary immunity (inviolability) of six opposition members were accepted by the Parliament.[143]

A November report notes the government elected in November 19 2002, 'has pledged to reject parliamentary immunity, which is meant to protect legislators from politically motivated charges but in fact has become a get-out-of-jail-free card." The report states that: "about 91 ousted members, now stripped of parliamentary immunity, face trial, most for abuse of power..."[144]

On September 5 2003, it was reported that the parliamentary commission chairman "stressing the determination of both the ruling Justice and Development party (A.K.) and the main opposition party Republican Peoples Party (C.H.P.) on lifting legislative immunities (inviolability). Currently there are 93 files on 54 deputies in Parliament waiting to be debated."[145]

However, two months later, it was reported that "while backing the anti-corruption campaign, opposition lawmakers... questioned the government's sincerity, pointing at its reluctance to limit the parliamentary immunity of legislators as means of cracking down on fraud.[146]

There was a disagreement within the parliamentary commission that deals with parliamentary immunity (inviolability), which had not met for nearly one year, about whether to close the meeting of the commission to the press. The commission members of both the ruling party (A.K.) and the opposition party (C.H.P.) eventually decided to hold the meeting in camera. The C.H.P. chairman accused the A.K. party of trying to postpone the parliamentary immunity (inviolability) files of A.K. party deputies, calling the A.K. party, "the party of those escaping justice." There were 57 files on A.K. party deputies and 51 files on C.H.P. deputies.[147]

The ruling party A.K. had not lifted parliamentary inviolability by the mid February, as promised, despite the main opposition party's pledge of support.[148]

UKRAINE

In september 2002, the Speaker of the Ukranian Supreme Rada, returned to the general prosecutor's office "a request to lift the parliamentary inviolability of leading oppositionist, Yulia Tymoshenko." The speaker said the request was "insufficiently motivated and short of well-substantiated specific facts. The prosecutor general opened a new (third) criminal case against Tymoshenko, and filed an official demand with the Rada to strip her of inviolability. Tymoshenko said she will ask the Rada to consent to her arrest or "give me an opportunity to work normally."[149]

In December 2004 the leader of "the Party of Industrialist and Entrepreneurs, who is a candidate in this year's presidential elections, is promising to initiate abolition of parliamentary deputies immunity (inviolability).... If he is elected as a president of Ukraine because it violates the principle of equality of all Ukrainian citizens before the law."[150]

Tom Warner of Financial Times in Kiev wrote in December, 2004

Volodymyr Lytvyn, the Speaker of <u>Ukraine's</u> parliament, said on Wednesday that court judges were being pressured to reverse a decision that stripped Volodymyr Satsyuk, deputy chief of the SBU secret police, of parliamentary immunity. Mr. Satsyuk, who is also a member of parliament, hosted a late-night meeting with Viktor Yushchenko, the opposition leader, hours before the latter's poisoning symptoms first appeared in early September.... The Kiev city appellate court ruled Tuesday that Mr. Satsyuk should be stripped of this parliamentary status, which had the effect of lifting his immunity to prosecution....But Leonid Kuchma, the outgoing president, is pushing to restore his ally's immunity, which could block any investigation of his conduct. Mr. Lytvyn, speaking in parliament on Wednesday, said the court's judges were being "pressured" to reverse their ruling, as Mr. Kuchma had signed a decree dismissing Mr. Satsyuk from his SBU job.[151]

VENEZUELA

In 2004 it was reported:

The Military Intelligence Directorate raided the home of [Democratic Action] Deputy Rafael Marin early on Tuesday morning [11 May], in violation of his parliamentary immunity (inviolability), arguing that he was in possession of documents linking him to the case of parliamentaries [arrested on 9 May in connection with alleged plot against President Hugo Chavez].[152]

YEMEN

It was reported on June 10, 2004 that:

> In an unusual precedent, the Yemeni parliament yesterday allowed about 2,000 women demonstrators-female students and school principals in the capital, Sanaa- to enter the parliament chamber to present a petition to lift the parliamentary immunity of two deputies from the Islamist-oriented Islah Party bloc. The demonstrators accused the two deputies of having called a number of women school principals infidels and of having defamed them.
>
> The event took place following a brief demonstration by the women in Tahrir Square, next to the parliament building, to demand that parliamentary immunity be lifted from Haza al-Masuri and Muhammad al-Hazmi, so that they could be tried by Yemeni courts.[153]

YUGOSLAVIA

In a 2002 story from Belgrade, Yugoslavia, the Associated Press wrote:

> The Yugoslav Parliament on Wednesday revoked the immunity of two lawmakers, who were associates of former Slobodan Milosevic, clearing the way for investigations into their wrongdoing during the former president's reign. Following a request by two Serbian courts, the federal assembly's lower chamber invalidated the immunity of Zoran Arandjelovic, a Socialist Party legislator, and that of Zivko Sokolovacki, a lawmaker from the communist Yugoslav Left party run by Milosevic's wife. Stripped of immunity as members of parliament, the two can now be prosecuted and tried in the courts of Serbia, Yugoslavia's larger republic.[154]

Chapter 7
Why it Matters that Parliamentary Inviolability Should End

This book has argued for the following proposition: Protection for the member beyond Parliament should be no more and no less than that provided to the rest of the citizenry. Inviolability and its attendant protection for the member erode the separation of powers. The Member like every citizen should appear before an independent judiciary following criminal charges laid by an independent prosecutorial authority. The independent prosecutorial arm of government should decide when to charge persons. The independent judiciary should provide an impartial ruling on the charges.

Parliament, of course, is the place where the member may make, with impunity, allegations of corruption and abuse of power in government and elsewhere. It is inconceivable today that a member would be criminally prosecuted for political activities alone. In Canada the ensuing ruckus in Parliament would be deafening. Members of all political stripes would not stand for it. Nor would the 'Fourth Estate'.

The patient reader may nod assent and say, yes, inviolability must be abolished and, yes, sooner than later. But in our troubled postmodern world does it really matter if parliamentary inviolability continues to be claimed by parliaments and parliamentarians?

We try to answer in this concluding chapter. I set the context with an observation by John Henry Newman who caught the world in a sentence:

> To consider the world in its length and breadth, its various history, the many races of man, their starts, their fortunes, their mutual alienation, their conflicts; and then their ways, habits, governments, forms of worship; their enterprises, their aimless courses, their random achievements and acquirements, the impotent conclusion of long-standing facts, the tokens so faint and broken of a superintending design, the blind evolution of what turns out to be great powers or truths, the progress of things, as if from unreasoning elements, not toward final causes, the greatness and littleness of man, his far-reaching aims, his short duration, the curtain hung over his futurity, the disappointments of life, the defect of good, the success of evil, physical pain, mental anguish, the prevalence and intensity of sin, the pervading idolatries, the corruptions, the dreary hopeless irreligion, that condition of the whole human race, so fearfully yet exactly described in the Apostle's words, 'having no hope and without God in the world,' – all this is a vision to dizzy and appall; and inflicts upon the mind the sense of a profound mystery which is absolutely beyond human solution.[*]

Perhaps the patient reader will applaud Newman's observation and say that is precisely the point. He or she may add that Marx, Sartre, Derrida, and Foucault are dead; that the drama of human atheism put into efficient, devastating, and deadly practice by Hitler and Stalin is behind us; that a reasonable person does not look to politicians alone for leadership or to politics for the answers to the big questions in life. So, she may repeat, does parliamentary inviolability really

---

[*] Apologia pro vita sua, John Henry Newman, Longman, Roberts and Green 1864, London.

matter? Does the rule of law, so very imperfectly realized to date in our troubled, fragmented world, really matter in the unfolding historical drama of the human enterprise?

I would reply to such a reader with a series of questions of my own. Who and what is the human person who claims for himself or herself the status of legal personhood requiring protection of life and liberty and demanding the freedom to develop human personhood in search of the true, the good, and the beautiful, possession of which should constitute personal fulfillment in personal happiness? Why bother with constitutions and charters and laws if, at bottom, this merely masks the futility of life that at its core is meaningless? Are our meanings merely arbitrary meanings we invent to cloak our reality as orphans in a universe devoid of meaning? If so, are human rights and the rule of law simply part of this papering over of our meaninglessness, a sort of intellectual cover up of our own abdication of the human mind's capacity for truth?

These questions are reasonable and fair and must be asked. It seems to me that reasonable and responsible human freedom requires that reasoning human persons accept personal responsibility to search for and find answers to these questions in the complex historical unfolding of the one human race. For our one humanity, in deep human solidarity, seeks a rule of law <u>with real meaning rooted in the truth of the intrinsic dignity of the human person and hence of that person's worth</u>. Otherwise, we must resign ourselves to live by what Professor Li Shuguang calls 'rule <u>by</u> law' and not the 'rule <u>of</u> law', the former 'serving merely as a tool for oppressive governments that suppress the human person in a legalistic way'.

Without seeking to add to the numerous concepts of human personhood and that acute problem of legal personhood, we may therefore insist that the question must be faced: What constitutes the intrinsic dignity of the human person that justifies our insistence that the rule of law does not mean mere rule by law? The answer may shed light on why the seemingly small step of abolition of parliamentary inviolability does really matter.

Let us start our answer with a fact: we do form but one human race on one planet earth. In the midst of plural economic, social, political, cultural, legal, religious, and spiritual communities, traditions, and histories, we are one humanity. And just as 'war is too important to be left to the generals', justice and the rule of law, both rooted in the intrinsic dignity of the human person, are too important to be left to politicians.

As the patient reader observed, we do not look to the politicians alone for leadership or to politics for the answers to the big questions of life. Indeed, politicians and politics merely keep the ship of state afloat to enable the rest of us, in the exercise of our human freedom, to find, or at least to search for, the meaning of life elsewhere.

This is no cynical disdain of politics or politicians, but a sober reminder of some distinctions a reasonable person may make. Undoubtedly, the meaning of life will not be found in politics. Certainly, human beings must take responsibility for their exercise of human freedom in search of meaning. This search, in the realm of political institutions, yields the find that politicians and technicians merely serve the state. Citizens direct it and this direction today espouses the rule of law.

Today, in the West, the world grows increasingly independent of the historical influence and power of the Church, a fact the Church accepts with its affirmation that it now merely proposes but does not impose. Whether the world has 'come of age' is another matter. But most certainly, at least since the Enlightenment, the world in its various intellectual disciplines and activities, in its sciences, arts, industries, and governments, continues to assert its independence of Church authority. By and large, this is to the world's credit in the secularized Western world at this time.

With such emancipation, however, as the world develops its own methods, techniques, and rules, there arises the need for a critically disciplined and reasonably rooted inquiry into the grounds for asserting the intrinsic dignity of the human person as foundation, norm, and end of human political society. This in turn gives rise to the need to distinguish between the empirical and the normative in the inescapable search for human meaning in the secularized Western world now working under its own steam to ground the rule of law in the intrinsic dignity of the human person.

The post-World War II development of human rights as a major preoccupation of public law highlights the importance of this task of deciphering the meaning of the human person as foundation, norm, and end of human political society. Parliamentary inviolability flies in the face of this development in human rights.

Consider the Universal Declaration of Human Rights adopted and proclaimed by the General Assembly of the United Nations on December 10, 1948, through Resolution 217A (III). Forty-eight states voted for the Declaration, and none voted against, but eight abstained: in alphabetical order, they are Czechoslovakia, Poland, Saudi Arabia, South Africa, Ukraine, U.S.S.R., White Russia, and Yugoslavia. With its seven whereas recitals in the Preamble and its thirty Articles, it was hailed as the constitution of the human rights movement. It is indeed a document that does honour to the skills of all persons involved in its negotiation, drafting and adoption, and is a document well worth reading and pondering. One notes its influence on the subsequent Canadian Charter of Rights and Freedoms.

Nonetheless, following its adoption, each state has placed its own interpretation on it. Some have even gone so far as to challenge its universality and to affirm the relativity of all human rights. Once again, the question of the meaning of 'human right' arises as we seek, as one humanity, to forge common understandings and common meanings. Words are necessary, but words alone do not give rise to such common understandings and meanings.

Consider simply the first recital of the Preamble and Articles 1 and 2 of the body of the Declaration:

Preamble

<u>Whereas</u> recognition of the inherent dignity and of the equal and inalienable rights of all members of the human family is the foundation of freedom, justice, and peace in the world.

<u>Article 1</u>

All human beings are born free and equal in dignity and rights. They are endowed with reason and conscience and should act toward one another in a spirit of brotherhood.

<u>Article 2</u>

Everyone is entitled to all the rights and freedoms set forth in this Declaration, without distinction of any kind, such as race, colour, sex, language, religion, political or other opinion, national or social origin, property, birth or other status.

Furthermore, no distinction shall be made on the basis of the political, jurisdictional, or international status of the country or territory to which a person belongs, whether it be independent, trust, non-self-governing, or under any other limitation of sovereignty.

The words are indeed memorable and strike a deep chord in the human psyche. Remarkable is the human achievement in negotiating, drafting, deliberating, revising, consulting, and reaching consensus in its adoption in our human fractured world, with its crazy quilt of colours and creeds*. Still, the need to strive to reach common understandings and meanings remains.

Consider simply the word "right", as an example. Every group, every movement, every brief to government, every Royal Commission, every cry for justice expresses a deep concern for rights. Let us, then, make a brief philosophic excursion into the meaning of "right" and "law".

Explore the historical evolution of these terms; such exploration discloses the divine, religious context from which the ideas spring.

The best Greek thinking stressed the teleology, the finality, the purposefulness of all things. This notion is inherent in the concepts "right" and "law". Indeed the word "right" and its equivalent in so many languages – "regte", "richte", "droit", "derecho" – all say "straight line". These two notions then, "religion" and "straight line", provide sure clues to the real meaning of "right". The divine is thus somehow mysteriously the beginning and the end. "Right" is thus somehow

---

* The record of UN debates shows that he (Malik, one of the draftspersons), tried strenuously to include an overt reference to natural law in wording of the Declaration. He proposed that the text read 'The family... is endowed by the Creator with inalienable rights antecedent to all positive law.' The debate over an explicit reference to God was even more fierce with regard to Article 1. Eventually the debate was reduced to two camps, one wanting to ground rights in "nature" and the other in God. In a kind of horse-trading arrangement, both proposed references were deleted in the final draft. ...yet we discern, in the doctrine of the Declaration, a partial and implicit return to the law of nature. A careful examination of the Preamble and Article 1 will reveal that the doctrine of natural law is woven at least into the intent of the declaration. (L'Humanité, Curle p. 41-2)

mysteriously the straight line (relation) of the human to the divine.

Even today, John Humphrey, one of the authors of the Universal Declaration of Human Rights, who regarded the UN's human rights project as the culmination of 'mankind's quest for a higher law, for some criteria higher than the law of the state', is of the view human rights represent the affirmation of human dignity based on the uniquely human capacity for relationship with the divine.[155]

This notion of "straight line" or finality was taken over and enriched by Christian thinkers to affirm that the relation of the human person to his or her destiny is the basic meaning of "right". And this relation is really understandable only within the religious context from which it springs* and is really rich only within the Christian context.

There arose also the notion of what is called "natural law". This too involved the notion of finality coupled with the notion of human nature. Thus the notion of human nature and the concept of the relation of human nature to the end or goal or fulfillment of that nature is called natural law. Hence, positive law, i.e., legislation, is the necessary concrete expression by human beings, legislators, of natural law to this particular

---

* As the reader saw in Chap. 3, when as westerners we foray into our past, we unavoidably encounter Christianity. It is perhaps difficult for us today to appreciate the extent to which Christian language and symbols permeated the thought of western thinkers from the beginning of the Christian period in the first century through to (and including!) the early modern period. All of life, including politics, was pondered in terms not separate from the Christian faith. The attempt has too seldom been made by contemporary political theorists to take seriously the Christian heritage of the west. Certainly this omission is due in part to the daunting task of gaining a working knowledge of the vast body of texts which inform the Christian tradition and which display an almost over-whelming variety of interpretations of that tradition. But it is also due to a certain discomfiture the typically secular academic of today shows towards religion, and traditional Christianily in particular, as a serious field of study for political philosophy or philosophy of law. (L'Humanité, Curle p. 53)

group at this particular time in this particular place. This does not mean syllogistic reasoning from a natural law 'substance' to the concrete here and now. It means rather that, while positive laws must constantly change from time to time and place to place in order better to serve the common good, legislators must never lose sight of the intrinsic dignity of the human person as they go about their important concrete tasks. While their practical judgments in enacting positive laws may constantly change, their prime duty as legislators must ever and always be to safeguard the only truly basic right of the human person, i.e., his or her relation to the end or fulfillment of the unique self, and the secondary or derived rights whereby no other person or persons or group or collectivity or society or state may hinder the human person from keeping on that straight line toward his or her final goal.

Fundamental right, therefore, in its most basic sense means straight line from the human person to God. The radical basis for all human rights is therefore the reality of the spiritual created nature of the human person and the relation of the person to God as his or her final destiny. Human right arises from the twofold duty of the human person, (1) to seek and possess the truth in its varied forms, and (2) to fulfill himself or herself in freedom and truth.

This fulfillment implies an order within, which should result in an order without, i.e., a hierarchy of inclinations, needs, and values rooted in the human person's very being and therefore rightly claiming the respect and support of government, whatever the form. For government is a means to an end. The end is the common good of the community, national and international. This means a Canadian and world atmosphere and social reality in which each person as person may seek fulfillment according to his or her unique personhood. Error has no rights, nor does truth, but only the human person because of his or her personal destiny to God.

Fundamental human right therefore derives from this twofold duty of the human person and gives rise to a duty, on the part of government, whatever the form, to give the human person his or her due as person.

The foregoing brief philosophic excursion into the radical or root basis of human right and natural law, as I understand it, should not sidetrack us from the complex reality of the historical human person. The human person is not only a spiritual created being ordained to God as final destiny, but an embodied historical being in search of human fulfillment in history. Nonetheless, a reasonable person who takes responsibility for personal freedom must ask and find an answer to the question, What is the human person and why is the person the foundation of the rule of law?

Pluralism in all its forms is a factual, historical, human reality. But at the heart and centre of our shared search for meaning is the meaning of the human person who transcends this pluralism. Our one human race cannot reasonably escape this search. The concept of the human person is at the heart and centre of all our human problems, and law is constitutive of the political-social organization of the human race in its plural manifestations. Indeed, law has several purposes: to regulate human conduct and not only to prevent certain consequences; to promote the common good (i.e., a social atmosphere and reality for the personal fulfillment of each human person); to educate the people and develop social values and attitudes; and to preserve life. But the several purposes of law and the dense complexity of the concrete order do not justify our avoiding the acute problem of legal personhood rooted in the human person as spiritual created being whence flows his or her intrinsic dignity and worth.

We may approach this in another way, by the route of justice rooted in the human person.

When we consider the principle of justice we cannot escape the two alternatives that face us head on: either the principle of justice is prior to the state, its constitution, covenants, and laws; or what is just or unjust is <u>completely</u> relative to the constitution of the state, dependent on its power, and a consequence of its laws.

This second alternative denies the existence of natural justice and the rule of law. It rejects the thrust of our brief philosophical excursion into the root basis of human right. It masquerades as rule of law but in reality is what professor Shuguang calls the rule <u>by</u> law, a tool for oppressive governments to suppress the human person. It also brings to mind the words of Felix Frankfurter: "Fragile as reason is and limited as law is as the institutional medium of reason, that's all we have standing between us and the tyranny of mere will and the cruelty of unbridled, undisciplined feeling."

The second alternative therefore denies the priority of justice. It also declares it either irrelevant or unknowable. It affirms an absolute autonomy for law rooted in the tyranny of mere will and the caprice of unfettered absolute power. On this approach, the government determines what is just or unjust, and the notion of fundamental human right rooted in the intrinsic dignity and worth of the human person is without meaning.

The first alternative, (i.e., the priority of the principle of justice), which I espouse, affirms the fundamental distinction between human right and legal right. Undoubtedly, in the historical concrete reality of human living, the justice of laws is <u>partly</u> relative to the constitution under which they are made and administered. But the constitution is not the ultimate standard of justice. The ultimate standard is not man-made but rooted in the human person itself as foundation, norm, and end of all human political society on earth. Some enactments violate the intrinsic dignity of the human person and thereby violate fundamental human justice and human right. They therefore can never be justified under any constitution.

We may also approach the problem from another angle, – the political, economic and ideological substructures underlying all human institutions. For example, the nation state is the basic concept of modern political thought and the "assembled nations" may more aptly describe what we call the United Nations.

Antiquity had its city states, the Middle Ages its universal empire, and the post-Reformation's new Europe brought with it separated states that gave rise to a new theory of state sovereignty that has bedeviled us ever since. Its growth from Bodin's <u>De Republica</u> in 1576, through Hobbes <u>Leviathan</u> in 1651, the advent of constitutional government, Locke and Rousseau, the American and French Revolutions in the eighteenth century, to nineteenth century national sentiment and the personification of the state as a sovereign juristic person which carried into the twentieth century and is our legacy as we begin the twenty-first – all this complex development presents a formidable problem for the rule of law founded upon the intrinsic dignity of the human person. For if sovereignty means absolute power and the modern state claims to be sovereign in the sense of a juristic person claiming absolute power, it cannot be <u>subject</u> to law. A state may <u>consent</u> to be bound by law, but cannot be <u>subjected</u> to law because of its sovereignty.

We have come a long way from Bodin for whom sovereignty was an essential legal principle of internal political order, and not of international disorder to prove that states by their very nature are above the law. We see here the practical realization of the rule <u>by</u> law in another manifestation. The absolute sovereign state determines what is just or unjust through the exercise of its unfettered absolute power. This claim obliterates the intrinsic dignity of the human person. Again, in this context, the rule of law faces a tremendous challenge. Again, the answer depends on our conception of the human person. Put Marxist thought into the equation and the two alternatives we discussed when dealing with the principle of justice may be stated thus: either the human person is autonomous in his or her spiritual created being and therefore not absorbed in the objective becoming of history; or the human person is not autonomous and must be absorbed in the objective becoming of history.

Here, further examples of the ideological substructures may assist our understanding of the importance of the human person as raison d'être of the state, its institutions, and the rule of law. Let us compare the theories of individualism and collectivism and their internal variations and external offshoots.[156]

Individualism in its various forms is difficult to define with accuracy. A reasonably safe generalization affirms that it sought to maximize individual freedom and minimize the state's activity to that of policeman and judge: to maintain order, enforce legal contracts, and protect individual freedom.

Its economic wing, which espoused unrestricted individualism in economic matters, included such notables as Adam Smith (1723-1790), Thomas Malthus (1776-1834), and David Ricardo (1772-1823) whose ideas profoundly affected subsequent economic practices rooted in so-called fixed, immutable "laws". The state must never tamper with these laws, they argued, but merely provide minimum sufficient order to permit these "laws" to operate unimpeded. The result was the extreme doctrine of laissez-faire which dominated the political thinking of the nineteenth century and sometimes masqueraded under the rubric "enlightened self interest".

Later on, individualism was brought to an extreme form based on the biological theory of evolution carried into the human-legal-social-political sphere by its leading proponent, the English philosopher Herbert Spencer (1820-1903). For Spencer, the state existed merely to guarantee individual rights and to ensure that only the fit survive. He opposed all forms of social welfare legislation with the following argument:

> It seems hard that a labourer incapacitated by sickness from competing with his stronger fellows, should have to bear the resulting privations. It seems hard that widows and orphans should be left to struggle for life or death. Nevertheless, when regarded not separately but in the interests of universal humanity, these harsh fatalities are seen to be full of the highest beneficence – the same beneficence which brings to early graves the children of diseased parents, and singles out the low-spirited, the intemperate, and the debilitated as the victims of an epidemic.[157]

Collectivism challenged individualism head on. Moving sharply away from nineteenth century laissez-faire thinking, it views government in a positive light as a vehicle for massive change in the social and economic life of its people. Its doctrinal and practical manifestations are socialism and communism. Like individualism they too come in many varieties. Their various forms are quite ambiguous and difficult to define with accuracy.

The Marxist variety of socialism, in turn, wears different dresses and may very broadly be divided between its revolutionary-violent wing (Lenin, Trotsky, Stalin) and its peaceful, non-violent wing (Bernstein and Bebel). The violent wing became known as communists, the peaceful wing as socialists.

The affirmation of the <u>truth</u> of the intrinsic dignity of the human person attempts to go beneath and beyond ideological thinking. It seeks to help us all rediscover the unconditional value of the person as created author and end of history, the foundation, norm and end of human political society. Without this, it seems to me, there can be no real hope for the effective realization of the rule of law. But with such rediscovery, a free, open, truthful confrontation of experiences, ideas and judgments among free people on a world scale may be possible, a dialogue in which there is no fear of any truth because of one's ideology, and no fear for one's ideology because of any truth.

This requires that governments be limited and controlled, as Madison well knew. In the <u>Federalist Papers</u>, James Madison pointed out that, "In framing a government which is to be administered by men over men, the great difficulty lies in this: you must first enable the government to control the governed; and in the next place oblige it to control itself."

From this angle, we may see the practical importance of the separation of powers (executive, legislative, judicial) and the need for a strong and independent judiciary not only as guardian of the constitution, (as modern theory still rooted at least tacitly in the sovereign state might put it), but, more importantly, as guardian of the life and liberty of the subject whose personhood enjoys intrinsic dignity and worth antecedently to the state, its constitution, laws, and covenants.

Brian Z. Tamanaha, author of <u>On the Rule of Law, History, Politics, Theory, 2001</u> wisely reminds us of certain realities to be kept in mind:

> Nowhere today can it be asserted plausibly that the government is just the community personified. The state system, and governments in their modern form, are of relatively recent invention no more than several centuries old, a development initially

of the West, which then spread by colonization or imitation. As such, the government has never been an extension of the community, at least not outside the imaginings of political theorists, but rather has everywhere been an institutionalized apparatus of concentrated power that constitutes the active operating mechanism of the state... The reality, demonstrated many times over, is that people in society have at least as much reason to fear the power wielded by government officials as they do to look forward to its fruits.[158]

The rule of law, therefore, takes on great importance as we attempt, as one humanity, to move beyond words alone to shared common understandings and common meanings. As I see it, the rule of law means not mere formal legality assuring regularity and consistency in the enforcement of order, but substantive justice based on the recognition that the human person is the foundation, the norm, and the end of human political society. Such recognition affirms the supreme value of the human person, as created spiritual being, unfolding in freedom his historical life on that straight line to God. Such recognition therefore supports and works for the development of institutions that provide a framework for the fullest expression of human personhood.

The rule of law therefore asserts that all persons are under it, both sovereign and subject, both leader and led, including the modern sovereign state. It rejects all arbitrariness and in particular arbitrary power. It asserts that the coercive power which the law must have at its command is not unlimited, that those who make and those who enforce the law are themselves subject to law, that there are ways of preventing them from abusing their power, and that an independent judiciary with an independent bar is a fundamental instrument in political society by which the rule of law can be made effective. In order to give effect to the rule of law, judges must hear the small as well as the great. This is not rule by judges but rather an affirmation that the judiciary is guardian not only of the constitution but of the life and liberty of the human person, whose intrinsic dignity is the created source of natural law and natural justice, antecedently to the constitution, laws, and covenants of the state.

Constitutions today must therefore be designed to govern governments; and the judiciary is a fundamental instrument for guarding the constitution. But the judiciary, at a deeper level, guards the human person in his intrinsic dignity and worth. Hence the whole citizenry needs to understand the reason why each human person enjoys such dignity antecedently to the constitution, laws, and covenants of the state, and antecedently to the judicial interpretations placed upon them.

The capacity of the human mind to affirm the truth is the key. This capacity allows us to affirm the truth of the spiritual created reality of the human person whence flows his and her intrinsic dignity. This capacity is the fundamental instrument of the one human race of human beings with personal, individual human minds. This capacity of the human mind functions "as a constraint on political power and a guide to our moral ends", to borrow from a related context the words uttered by Hadley Arkes, Edward Ney Professor of Jurisprudence and American Institutions at Amherst College..

There is, then, a seamless web of interconnected notions in the study or parliamentary inviolability. They include the state, government, society, the separation of powers, the role of parliament, the role of the judiciary, the principle of justice, and the rule of law as opposed to the rule by law. But underlying all this is the capacity of the human mind to know reality and thereby to affirm the truth about the intrinsic dignity and worth of the human person.

Madison knew the truth about this intrinsic dignity. The Declaration of Independence enunciates it with eloquent clarity. But the practical measures required in framing a constitution presented complex problems. He puts his finger on the great practical difficulty in framing a government: first, enable the government to control the governed; next, oblige it to control itself.

These pages simply extend an invitation to parliaments and parliamentarians, especially the European Parliament, to control themselves by abolishing parliamentary inviolability. Do they still claim to need protection from the executive? Do they still claim to require protection from false and ill-founded proceedings brought for political reasons? Do they still require protection from "la puissance des baïonnettes?" Do they really espouse the rule of law for all when they continue to claim for themselves a special immunity from prosecution or detention?

Yes, it matters that parliamentary inviolability be abolished sooner than later, if only because one of Europe's new challenges is to make the European Union an area of freedom, security, and justice where everyone has *equal* access to justice and is equally protected by the law.* As of May 1st, 2004, nearly half a billion human beings in the then 15 members of the European Union have chosen to live under the rule of law and in accordance with age-old values that centre on humanity and human dignity.

Members of the European Parliament need to screw up their courage by stepping off their pedestals and rejecting the mantle of inviolability when they are outside Parliament among their fellow citizens and electors. Inviolability constantly intrudes upon modern constitutionalism, the separation of powers, and the rule of law. It erodes the citizens' rightful expectation in a modern democracy that everyone is equal

---

* Europe in 12 Lessons, European Commission 2003, p. 4, emphasis added.

before the law. It encourages disrespect for and clashes among the three branches of government as the Juppé affair in France and the Berlusconi affair in Italy amply demonstrate. One must wonder and ask: Are the member states of the European Union not functioning democracies? Do they not claim to live by the rule of law?

Twenty seven sovereign states now comprise the European Union and membership in the European Parliament. After two terrible wars that constituted an abattoir on European soil and beyond, international pressures and diplomacy brought about declarations, covenants, and conventions promoting human, civil, and political rights. With the end of the Cold War, conventions on the Rule of law were adopted world wide. According to the Inter-Parliamentary Symposium Report, Guardian of Human Rights, 1993, 'nearly 200 states now make up the international community. Two thirds of them have been in existence for less than 40 years.' Is it too much to ask that the European Parliament stiffen its spine to show the lead as 'guardians of human rights'? But how can it do this if it continues the charade of insisting on parliamentary inviolability for its own members?

In this connection, I admire those two "newest states", South Africa and East Timor. The Constitution of the Republic of South Africa (1996) provides for immunity in Parliament according to the Westminster model. Although coming from a continental European (Portugal) tradition, the East Timor Constitution does likewise. I was involved in East Timor's consultations. In the autumn of 2001 I advised the members of their Constituent Assembly to follow the Westminster model. I suggested that, as the newest independent state, they could set an example for the world by providing for immunity in their constitution without claiming inviolability. This courageous and resilient people agreed, to their profound credit. What of the European Parliament? Are its members not up to the task?

While at least the United States of America and the United Kingdom were raised on the parliamentary immunity model, rather than inviolability, the Western authorities yet missed a golden opportunity to advance the cause for good governance when they were involved in drafting the new constitutions for Afghanistan and Iraq. They provided parliamentary inviolability for the parliamentarians, rather than parliamentary immunity. Does this advance the rule of law?

Jettisoning the claim to inviolability is not a panacea. This will not cure all the ills of bad governance. It is only one step among many to good governance. But it is an essential step for parliamentarians worldwide who seek to claim, <u>with transparency and integrity</u>, their earnest and genuine desire to promote the rule of law today. It is a concrete practical step to raise the hopes of people everywhere.

I am not unaware of the vicissitudes of human life, the dense complexity of human nature, the catastrophes of human history, and the difficult quest for human meaning in the ongoing unfolding of the mysterious human species down the centuries. Là où il y a de l'homme, il y a de l'hommerie. Nonetheless, at the table of good governance, parliamentary inviolability can no longer credibly claim a seat among those who genuinely seek to advance the rule of law on planet earth.

Of course, I cannot oblige them to control themselves by abolishing parliamentary inviolability. We may only hope parliamentarians will accept an invitation by taking this practical step as tangible and concrete sign of their faithful commitment to the rule of law and the equality of all before the law.

And so, as meagre as this contribution may appear to some, and perhaps in reality may be, I believe it does matter in a secularist age in search of common understandings and common meanings to affirm the meaning of the human person, as foundation, norm and end of human political society.

This is an appeal to all politicians everywhere, but particularly to politicians of the European Parliament. Take the small step it advocates. Encourage and act for the abolition of parliamentary inviolability as a concrete sign of genuine espousal of the rule of law. Who knows? It may have implications for peace in this world.

Bibliography

1215 the Year of Magna Carta, by Danny Danziger & Gillingham, Hodder & Stouton, London,2003

A Constitutional History of the House of Lords, from original sources, Luke Owen Pike, 1894, Macmillan and Co, London

An Encyclopedia of Parliament, N. Wilding & P. Laundy, 4ed, 1972, Cassell, London

Anecdotal History of the British Parliament from the earliest Period, 4th ed., G.H. Jennings, London, Horace Cox, 1899

A History of English Law, Sir William Holdsworth, vol. I to XV, plus Index (vol. XVI I) Methuen & Cohto, London

Angevin Kingship, J.E.A. Joliffe, 1963, Adam & Charles Black, London

Appearing for the Crown, A Legal and Historical Review of Criminal Prosecutorial Authority in Canada, Philip C. Stenning, A study conducted for the Law Reform Commission of Canada, 1986, Brown Legal Publications, Inc./Les Éditions Yvon Blais, Cowansville, Québec, Canada

Commentaries on the Laws of England, 8ed, William Blackstone, Press 1778, Oxford: Clarendon 1986

Constitutional History of England, vol. I to III, 6ed, WimStubbs, Oxford, Clarendon Press

Constitutional Law in Theory and Practice, David Beatty, University of Toronto Press, Toronto, Buffalo, London, 1995

Constitutionalism: Ancient and Modern, C.H. McIlwain, Cornell Paperbacks, Cornell University Press, Ithaca, London, revised ed., 1947

Controlling the English Prosecutor, by Douglas Hay, Osgoode Hall Law Journal, June 1983

Constitutions of the Countries of the World, Oceana Publications, Dobbs Ferry, New York, USA

Convention for the Protection of Human Rights & Fundamental Freedoms, as mended by Protocol no. 11, Rome 1950

Crime and Punishment in Eighteenth Century England, Frank McLynn, Routledge, London & New York, 1989

English Social History, A Survey of Six Centuries, Chaucer to Queen Victoria, by G. M. Trevelyan, 1942, Longmans, Green & Co., London, NY, Toronto

Europe in 12 Lessons, by Pascal Fontaine (former assistant to Jean Monnet), European Commission, 2003 Brussels

Guardian of Human Rights, Parliament's Responsibility and Role in Ensuring That Human Rights and the Rights of Minorities are Respected and Protected; Human Rights and Parliamentary Immunities, IPU Symposium Report, Budapest, May 1993

Historical Studies of the English Parliament, E.B. Fryde & Edward Miller, ed. 1970, Cambridge University Press, vol. I-II

How the European Union Works, A citizen's guide to the European Union institutions, European Commission, 2003 Bruxelles

L'Immunité parlementaire dans les états membres de l'Union Européen, 1996, document de travail, Parlement Européen Luxembourg, par Marilia Crespo Allen

Internal Stury of the European Parliament's Parliamentary Imminity in the European Parliament, 2005

Les constitutions de la France, M. Faustin-Adolphe Hélie, A. Maresco Ainé, libraire-éditeur, Paris, 1875

Les parlementaires et la justice : la procédure de suspension de la détente, des mesures privatives ou restrictive de liberté, et de la poursuite, Patrick Fraisseix, 39 Revue française de droit constitutional, 1999, p. 498

Les immunités parlementaires en droit camerounais : réflexion sur une exception au principe de l'égalité des citoyens devant la loi, Célestin Keutcha Tchapnga, assistant à la faculté des sciences juridiques et politiques de l'université de Dschang, Revue Juridique et Politique : Indépendance et Coopération, vol. 52, 1998

L'Humanité, John Humphrey's alternative account of human rights, Clinton Timothy Carle, University of Toronto Press, 2006

Magna Carta, J.C. Holt, Cambridge University Press, 1965

Magna Carta, the Heritage of Liberty, Anne Palliser, 1971, Clarendon Press

May's Parliamentary Practice, ed C.J. Boulton Butterworth 21ed, 1989,

Parliament and the Police: the Saga of Bill C-79, James Robertson and Margaret Young, Canadian Parliamentary Review, Winter, 1991-1992

Parliamentary Privilege in Canada, 2ed, 1997, J.P. Joseph Maingot, QC, House of Commons and McGill-Queen's University Press, Montréal, Canada

On The Rule of Law, History, Politics, Theory, Brian Z. Tamanaha, 2004, Cambridge University Press

Parliaments in the Modern World, Philip Laundy, IPU, Darmouth Publishing, 1989

Parliaments of the World, A Comparative Reference Compendium 1986, 2ed, vol. I, Inter-Parliamentary Union, the Inter-parliamentary Centre for Parliamentary Documentation of the Inter-Parliamentary Union

Precedents of Proceedings in the House of Commons, John Hatsell, 4th ed, vol. I, 1818; Rothman Reprints Inc, N.J., 1971

Privileges and Immunities of Members of the European Parliament, Select Committee of the European Communities, House of Lords, HL105

Protocol on the Privileges and Immunities of the European Communities, of 8 April 1965, Report on the Regime of Parliamentary Immunity, Venice Commission, Strasbourg, 4 June 1996 (IPU)

Revue Française de Droit Constitutionnel, 1994, vol. 20; 1999, vol. 39

Roman Civilization, Selected Readings, ed. by Naphtali Lewis and Meyer Reinhold, vol. I, 3ed, 1990, Columbia University Press, NY, NY

Rules on Parliamentary Immunity in European Parliament and the Member States of the European Union (final draft), 2001, European Parliament

Textes constitutionnels révolutionnaires français, Michel Verreaux, Imprimerie des Presses, Universitaires de France, 1998

The Crisis of Church and State, 1050-1300, Brian Tierney, University of Toronto Press, 1988

The High Court of Parliament and Its Supremacy, an Historical Essay on the Boundaries between Legislation and Adjudication in England, C.H. McIlwain, 1910, Yale University Press, Archon Books, Hamden, Connecticut, 1962

The History of Government from the Earliest Times, vol. III, Empires, Monarchies and the Modern State, S. E. Finer, Oxford University Press, 1997

The History of Iceland, Gunnar Karlsson, University of Minnesota Press, Minneapolis, 2000

The House of Lords from Saxon Wargods to a Modern Senate, John Wells, Hodder and Stoughton, 1997, London

The House of Lords in the Middle Ages, Enoch Powell and Keith Wallis, 1968, Weidendeld and Nicolson, London

Immunités parlementaires ou impunité de parlementaire, Hervé Issar, 20 Revue française de droit constitutional, 1994, p.675

The Immunities of Members of Parliament, Robert Myttenaere, 1998, Inter Parliamentary Union, Moscow Session

The Limits of Immunity: Principle and Practice, by Christian Kopetzki, Department of Public Law, University of Vienna, Austria Today, vol. 4, 1998

The Making of Europe: Conquest, Colonization and Cultural Change, 950-1350, Robert Bartlett, 1993, Princeton University Press, Princeton, New Jersey

The Office of the Speaker in the Parliaments of the Commonwealth, Philip Laundy, Quiller Press Ltd., London, 1986

The Parliament of Canada, C.S. Franks, 1987, University of Toronto Press

The Parliamentary Mandate, A Global Comparative Study, Marc Van der Hulst, Inter Parliamentary Union, 2000

The Procedure of the House of Commons, A Study of Its History and Present Form, Josef Redlich, vol. I-III, 1908, AMS Press, New York, translated from the German by A. Ernest Stenthal

Western Society and the Church in the Middle Ages, R.W. Southern, Pelican Books, The Pelican History of the Church, vol. 2, 1990, p. 99

World Encyclopaedia of Parliaments and Legislature, Congressional Quarterly Inc, Washington. D.C., 1998

Annex 1

List of world parliaments whose constitutions or legislation provide for parliamentary inviolability or immunity, and where it is unclear because of lack of information

Inviolability	Immunity	Unclear
Afghanistan	Antigua	Lesotho
Albania	Australia	Zimbabwe
Algeria	The Bahamas	Swaziland
Andorra	Bangladesh	Grenada
Angola	Barbados	Uganda
Argentina	Belize	
Armenia	Bhutan	
Austria	Bosnia & Herzegovina	
Azerbaijan	Botswana	
Bahrain	Brunei Darussalam	
Belarus	Canada	
Belgium	Columbia	
Benin	Dominica	
Bolivia	East Timor	
Brazil	Fiji Islands	
Bulgaria	the Gambia	
Burkina Faso	Ghana	

Inviolability	Immunity	Unclear
Burundi	Guyana	
Cambodia	India	
Cameroon	Iran	
Cape Verde	Ireland	
Central African Republic	Jamaica	
Chad	Kenya	
Chile	Kiribati	
China	Malawi	
Comoros	Maldives	
Congo	Malta	
Costa Rica	Mauritius	
Côte d'Ivoire	Namibia	
Croatia	Nauru	
Cuba	The Netherlands	
Cyprus	New Zealand	
Czech Republic	Nigeria	
Denmark	Pakistan	
Dji Bouti	Papua New Guinea	
Dominica Republic	St. Christopher & Nevis	
Ecuador	St. Lucia	
Egypt	St. Vincent	
El Salvador	Sierra Leone	
Equatorial Guinea	Singapore	
Eritrea	Solomon Islands	
Estonia	South Africa	
Ethiopia	Sri Lanka	
the European Parliament	Suriname	
Finland	Tanzania	

Inviolability	Immunity	Unclear
France	Thailand	
Gabon	Tonga	
Georgia	Trinidad & Tobago	
Germany	Tuvalu	
Greece	U.K.	
Guatemala	U.S.A.	
Guinea	Zambia	
Guinea-Bissau		
Haïti		
Honduras		
Hungary		
Iceland		
Indonesia		
Iraq		
Israel		
Italy		
Japan		
Jordan		
Korea, Democratic People's Republic		
Korea, Republic		
Kuwait		
Kyrgyz Republic		
Laos		
Latvia		
Lebanon		
Liberia		

Inviolability	Immunity	Unclear
Libya (no constitution or legislature since overthrow of King Idris in 1969)		
Liechtenstein		
Lithuania		
Luxembourg		
Macedonia		
Madagascar		
Malaysia		
Mali		
Marshall Island		
Mauritania		
Mexico		
Micronesia		
Moldova		
Monaco		
Mongolia		
Morocco		
Mozambique		
Myanmar (Burma) – as of 1988 the country's govt is controlled by the State Law & Restoration Council		
Nepal		
Nicaragua		
Niger		
Norway		
Oman – based on Islamic Sharia		
Palau		

Inviolability	Immunity	Unclear

Panama

Paraguay

Peru

Philippines

Poland

Portugal

Qatar (constitution provides
for a Ruler, a Council of
Ministers and an Advisory
Council

Romania

Russian Federation

Rwanda

Samao

Sâo Tomé; Principe

Saudi Arabia – the Sharia
rules & provides basic Islamic
system

Senegal

Serbia/Montenegro

Seychelles

Slovakia

Slovenia

Somalia – no elected govt. or
constitution at present

Spain

Sudan

Sweden

Switzerland

Syria

Inviolability	Immunity	Unclear
Taiwan		
Tajikistan		
Togo		
Tunisia		
Turkey		
Turkmenistan		
Ukraine		
United Arab Emirates		
Uruguay		
Uzbekistan		
Vanuatu		
Venezuela		
Vietnam		
Yemen		

Annex 2

Constitutions of Countries of the World[159] Provisions Relating to Parliamentary Inviolability or Immunity, and where appropriate, including legislation pursuant to the constitution

Afghanistan (1382-2003)

Article 101

No member of the National Assembly shall be legally prosecuted for expressing his views while performing his duties.

Article 102

When a member of the National Assembly is accused of a crime, the law enforcement authority informs the House of which the accused member is about the case, and the accused member can be prosecuted.

In case of an evident crime, the law enforcement authority can legally pursue and arrest the accused without the permission of the House, which the accused is a member of. In both cases, when legal prosecution requires detentions of the accused, law enforcement authorities are obligated to inform the respective House about the case immediately.

If the accusation takes place when the National Assembly is in recess, the permission of arrest is obtained from the administrative committee of the respective House and the decision of this committee shall be presented to the first session of that House for a decision.

Albania (1998)

Article 73

1. A Deputy does not bear responsibility for opinions expressed in the Assembly and votes given. This provision is not applicable in the case of defamation.

2. A Deputy may not be criminally prosecuted without the authorization of the Assembly. Authorization is also required when he is to be arrested.

3. A Deputy may be detained or arrested without authorization when he is apprehended during or immediately after the commission of a serious crime. In these cases, the General Prosecutor immediately notifies the Assembly, which, when it determines that the proceeding is misplaced, decides to lift the measure.

Algeria (1989)

Article 109

Parliamentary immunity is granted to the deputies and to the members of the Council of the Nation during the term of their mandate.

They may not be prosecuted, arrested, or in general be the object of civil of criminal action nor all forms of pressure, on account of opinions expressed, speeches delivered or votes cast in the exercise of their mandate.

Article 110

The prosecutions *[poursuites]* for a delinquent act against a deputy or a member of the Council or the Nation may not be initiated *[engagées]* except by express renunciation *[renonciation]* of the concerned *[l'interessé]* or upon authorization in each case by the National People's Assembly or the Council of the Nation which decides by a majority of its members the lifting of their *[son]* immunity.

Article 111

In case of a flagrant offense or flagrant crime the deputy or a member of the Council of the Nation, the arrest can proceed. The bureau of the National People's Assembly or the Council of the Nation must be informed immediately.

Andorra (1993)

Article 53

2. The Councillors may not be called to account for votes cast or any utterances made in the exercise of their functions.

3. Throughout their term the Councillors may not be arrested or detained, except in the cases of flagrante delicto. But for that case, their detention and prosecution shall be decided by the plenary session of the Tribunal de Corts and the trial shall be held by the Higher Court.

Angola (1975-1980)

MPLA
Article 48

No deputy of the People's Assembly may be arrested without charge or taken to court without the authorization of the Assembly or of its Permanent Commission, except in cases of flagrante delicto for a heinous crime carrying a major sentence.

Article 51

The Permanent Commission shall answer to the People's Assembly, and shall periodically present reports on its activities.

UNITA
Article 49

(Immunities)

1. No deputy will answer civilly, criminally or disciplinarily for deeds resulting from the exercise of his duties.

2. Deputies cannot be arrested or held, without the authorization of the National Assembly, except in flagrante delicto or definitive sentencing for a felony.

Antigua (1981)

Article 58

1. Without prejudice to any provision made by Parliament relating to the powers, privileges and immunities of Parliament and its committees, or the privileges and immunities of the members and officers of either House of Parliament and of other persons concerned in the business of Parliament or its committees, no civil or criminal proceedings may be instituted against any member of either House of Parliament for words spoken before, or written in a report to, the House of Parliament of which he is a member or a committee thereof or any joint committee of the senate and the House or by reason of any matter or thing brought by him therein by petition, bill, resolution, motion or otherwise.

Argentina (1994)

Article 68

No member of Congress may be indicted, judicially questioned, or harassed for the opinions expressed or speeches made by him in the performance of his duties as a legislator.

Article 69

No Senator or Deputy, from the day of his election until he leaves office, may be arrested, except in case of his being caught **in flagrante** in the commission of a capital or other infamous or grave crime, in which case a summary report of the facts shall be made to the appropriate Chamber.

Article 70

When a written charge is presented before the ordinary courts against any Senator or Deputy, each Chamber, after examining the merits of the indictment in public trial, may by a two thirds vote suspend the accused from his office and place him at the disposal of the proper court for trial.

Armenia (1995)

Article 66

A Deputy shall not be bound by any compulsory mandate and shall be guided by his or her conscience and convictions. A Deputy shall not be prosecuted or held liable for the actions arising from the performance of his or her status, or for the expression of his or her opinions expressed in the National Assembly, provided these are not slanderous or defamatory.

A Deputy may not be arrested and subjected to administrative or criminal prosecution through judicial proceedings without the consent of the National Assembly.

Australia (1901-1986)

Article 49

The powers, privileges, and immunities of the Senate and of the House of Representatives, and of the members and the committees of each House, shall be such as are declared by the Parliament, and until declared shall be those of the Commons House of Parliament of the United Kingdom, and of its members and committees, at the establishment of the Commonwealth.

Austria (1920-2002)

Article 57

(1) The members of the National Council may never be made responsible for votes cast in the exercise of their function and only by the National Council on the grounds of oral or written utterances made in the course of their function.

(2) The members of the National Council may on the ground of a criminal offense – the case of apprehension in the act of committing a crime excepted – be arrested only with the consent of the National Council. Likewise,

searches of houses of members of the National Council require the consent of the National Council.

(3) Otherwise members of the National Council may only be officially prosecuted on account of a punishable act, with the consent of the National Council, if it has obviously no connection with the official activity of the deputy in question. However, the agency *[Behorde]* must seen a ruling from the National Council concerning the existence of such a connection if the concerned deputy or a third of the members of the Standing Committee [which is] entrusted with these matters, demand it. In case of such a demand, any official prosecuting action must immediately cease or be terminated.

(4) The consent of the National Council must be deemed granted in all these cases, if the National Council has not given a ruling within eight weeks to the request by the agency which is competent to initiate the prosecution. In order to meet the deadline date *[Rechtzeitig]* for a ruling by the National Council, the President [of the National Council] must call for a vote at the latest one the day before the expiration of the deadline. The time when [the National Council] is not in session is not included in the deadline.

(5) In case of apprehension in the act of committing a crime, the agency must immediately notify the President of the National Council of the executed arrest. If the National Council, or, during the session-free time, the Standing Committee which is entrusted with these matters, demands it, the arrest much be lifted and the prosecution dropped altogether.

(6) The immunity of the deputies ends on the day of the convening of the National Council, [the immunity] of organs of the National Council, whose functions extend beyond this point in time [ends] with the expiration of this function.

Article 58

The members of the Federal Council enjoy during the entire duration of their functions the immunity of members of the *Land* legislature, which has sent them.

Azerbaijan (2002)

Article 90

The Immunity of the Deputy of the Milli Mejlis of the Azerbaijan Republic

I. The Deputy of the Milli Mejlis of the Azerbaijan Republic during the term of office has personal immunity. With the exception of cases when he has been caught in flagrante delicto, the Deputy during the term of office cannot be brought to court, detained, administrative measures of punishment cannot be applied to him. He cannot be arrested or punished in some other way, he cannot be searched, examined. The Deputy of the Milli Mejlis of the Azerbaijan Republic can be detained if caught in flagrante delicto. In this case the organ which has detained the Deputy of the Milli Mejlis of the Azerbaijan Republic must inform the General Procurator of the Azerbaijan Republic.

II. The Immunity of the Deputy of the Milli Mejlis of the Azerbaijan Republic can be terminated only by the decision of the Milli Mejlis of the Azerbaijan Republic on the basis of proposals of the Milli Mejlis of the Azerbaijan Republic by the General Procurator.

The Bahamas (1973-2002)

Article 53

(1) Without prejudice to the generality of Article 52(1) of this Constitution and subject to the provisions of paragraph (2) of this Article, Parliament may by law determine the privileges, immunities and powers of the Senate and the House of Assembly and the members thereof.

(2) No process issued by any court in the exercise of its civil jurisdiction shall be served or executed within the precincts of the Senate or the House of Assembly while it is sitting, or through the President or the Speaker, the Clerk or any other officer of either House.

Powers and Privileges (Senate and House of Assembly) Act, Ch. 8

An Act to amend and consolidate the law relating to the privileges, immunities and powers of the Senate and the House of Assembly and Senators and the Members of the said House, and for purposes incidental thereto or connected therewith.

3. Senators and Members shall have the like privileges and immunities as are enjoyed for the time being in the United Kingdom by members of the Commons House of Parliament, and without derogation from the generality of the privileges and immunities conferred by this section, in particular shall have such privileges and immunities as are provided hereafter in this Act.

4. No civil or criminal proceedings may be instituted against any Senator or Member for words spoken before, or written in a report to, the Senate or the House respectively or a committee, or by reason of any matter or thing so brought by him by petition, bill, motion or otherwise.

5. No Senator or Member shall be liable to arrest –
   (a) for any civil debt whilst going to, attending at or returning from any sitting of the Senate or the House respectively or any committee;
   (b) within the precincts of the Senate of the House while the Senate or the House or a committee is sitting, for any criminal offence, without the consent of the President or the Speaker, as the case may be.

Bahrain (2002)

Article 89

    b. No member of the Consultative Council or the Chamber of Deputies shall be called to account for expressing his opinions or ideas in the Council of its committees unless the opinion expressed is prejudicial to the fundamentals of the religion or the unity of the nation, or the mandatory respect for the King, or is defamatory of the personal life of any person.

    c. Other than in case of *flagrante delicto*, it shall be impermissible during the convening period for any detention, investigation, search, arrest or custodial procedures or any other penal action to be taken against a member except with the permission of the chamber of which he is a member. Outside the convening period, permission must be sought from the President or the relevant chamber.

The non-issue of a decision by the chamber or its President on the permission which is being sought within one month from the date of receipt of the request shall be regarded as permission.

The chamber must be informed of any measures which may be taken under the preceding paragraph while it is convened, and it must invariably be informed at its first session of any action taken against a member during the chamber's annual recess.

Bangladesh (1972-1996)

Article 78

    (1) The validity of the proceedings in Parliament shall not be questioned in any court.

    (2) A member or officer of Parliament in whom powers are vested for the regulation of procedure, the conduct of business of the maintenance of order in Parliament, shall not in relation to the exercise by him of any such powers be subject to the jurisdiction of any court.

(3) A member of Parliament shall not be liable to proceedings in any court in respect of anything said, or any vote given, by him in Parliament or in any committee thereof.

(4) A person shall not be liable to proceedings in any court in respect of the publication by or under the authority of Parliament of any report, paper, vote or proceeding.

(5) Subject to this article, the privileges of Parliament and its committees and members may be determined by Act of Parliament.

Barbados (1966-1996)

Article 48

(7) Without prejudice to the generality of subsection (1) and subject to the provisions of subsection (3), Parliament may by law determine the privileges, immunities and powers of the Senate and the House of Assembly and the members thereof.

Chapter 9. Parliament (Privileges, Immunities and Powers) Immunities

4. No civil or criminal proceedings may be instituted against any member

   (a) in respect of words spoken before; or

   (b) in respect of words written in a report to; or

   (c) by reason of any matter or thing brought by petition, bill, motion or otherwise, before the House to which he belongs, or to a committee thereof, or a joint committee.

5. (1) No member shall, during a session, be liable to arrest or imprisonment on any civil process, except for a debt the contraction of which constitutes a criminal offence.

Belarus (1996)

Article 102

The Deputies of the Chamber of Representatives and members of the Council of the Republic enjoy immunity in the expression of their views and exercise of their powers. This does not refer to charges of slander and insult.

Belgium (1831)

Article 58

No member of either of the two Chambers may be prosecuted or sought out as a result of the opinions and votes expressed in the exercise of his functions.

Article 59

(As amended Feb. 28, 1997)

During the session, except in case of *flagrante delicto*, a member of either of the two Chambers may only be prosecuted or arrested in penal matters [*matière répressive*] with the permission of the Chamber, [and] turned over to a court or a tribunal.

Except in the case of apprehension [*flagrante delicto*], for coercive measures against a member of either Chamber, the intervention of a Judge is required, while during the session period in penal matters [*matière répressive*] can be ordered only by the first President of the Court of Appeals, on the demand of the competent judge. This decision is communicated to the President of the concerned Chamber.

A search [*perquisition*] of seizure, on the basis of the preceding paragraph, may be carried out only in the presence of the President of the concerned Chamber or by a member designated by him.

During the session period only the officers of the Public Prosecutor or the competent agents may initiate prosecution in penal matters against a member of either Chamber. During the session period in penal matters, at each stage of the investigation, the concerned member of either Chamber may demand the suspension of the prosecution.

The concerned Chamber must decide with a two-thirds majority of all the votes.

The detention of a member of either Chamber or his prosecution before a court of tribunal is suspended during the session if the Chamber of which he is a member, demands it.

Belize (1981-1988)

Article 74

Without prejudice to any provision made by the National Assembly relating to the powers, privileges and immunities of the Senate or the House of Representatives and the committees thereof, or the privileges and immunities of the members and officers of either House and of other persons concerned in the business of either House of the committees thereof, no civil or criminal proceedings may be instituted against any member of either House for words spoken before, or written in a report to, either House or a committee thereof or by reason of any matter or thing brought by him therein by petition, Bill, resolution, motion or otherwise.

Republic of Benin (1990)

Article 90

The members of the National Assembly shall enjoy parliamentary immunity. As a consequence, no Deputy may be followed, searched, arrested, detained or judged for opinions or votes issued by him during the exercise of his duties.

A Deputy may, during the duration of the sessions, be followed or arrested in a criminal or correctional matter only with the authorization of the National Assembly except in the case of a flagrant offense.

A Deputy outside of the session may be arrested only with the authorization of the Office of the National Assembly, except n the case of a flagrant offense, of authorized legal actions or of final conviction.

The detention or pursuit of a Deputy shall be suspended if the National Assembly should require it for a vote by a two-thirds majority.

Bhutan (1953)

Rule No. 11

Every Member shall have the full right and privilege to express his thoughts in the Assembly. No rule or law can interfere with a Member's freedom of expression.

Bolivia (1967)

Article 51

Deputies and senators are inviolable at all times for the opinions expressed by them in the discharge of their duties.

Article 52

No senator or deputy shall be accused, prosecuted, or arrested in any matter from the day of his election continuously until the end of his term of office unless the chamber to which he belongs consents by a two-thirds vote. In civil matters he may not be sued or required to give bond during a period beginning sixty days before the meeting of Congress and ending at the time he returns to his residence.

Article 53

The vice president of the republic, in his capacity of president of the national Congress and of the Senate, enjoys the same immunities and prerogatives granted to senators and deputies.

Bosnia and Herzegovina (1995)

Article 3

j. Delegates and Members shall not be held criminally or civilly liable for any acts carried out within the scope of their duties in the Parliamentary Assembly.

Botswana (1966)

Article 86

Subject to the provisions of this Constitution, Parliament shall have power to make laws for the peace, order and good government of Botswana.

CAP. 02:03 National Assembly (Powers and Privileges)

3. No civil or criminal proceedings may be instituted against any Member for words spoken before, or written in a report to, to Assembly or to a committee, or by reason of any matter or thing to brought to him by petition, Bill, motion or otherwise.

4. No Member shall be liable to arrest –

   (a) for any civil debt whilst going to, attending at or returning from a sitting of the Assembly or any committee; or

   (b) within the precincts of the Assembly while the Assembly or a committee is sitting for any criminal offence, without the consent of the Speaker.

Brazil (1992-2002)

Article 53

The Deputies and Senators shall enjoy civil and criminal immunity for any of their opinions, words and votes.

1°. From the date of their investiture, Deputies and Senators shall be judged by the Supreme Federal Tribunal.

2°. From the date of their investiture, members of the National Congress may not be arrested, except in flagrante delicto, for anon-bailable crime. In this case, the police record shall be sent within twenty-four hours to the respective Chamber, which, by majority vote of its members, shall decide as to imprisonment.

3°. When an accusation has been received against a Senator of Deputy for a crime committed after investiture, the Supreme Federal Tribunal shall notify the respective Chamber, which, by initiative of a political party represented therein and by a majority vote of its members, may, until the final decision, suspend the proceedings in the case.

4°. Upon receipt by the Executive Committee, a request for a suspension shall be acted upon by the respective Chamber during a non-extendable period of forty-five days.

5°. A suspension shall toll the running of the limitations period for the duration of the mandate.

8°. Immunity of Deputies or Senators shall continue during a state of siege and may be suspended only by vote of two-thirds of the members of the respective Chamber, in cases of acts performed outside the premises of Congress that are incompatible with the implementation of such a measure.

Brunei Darussalam (1984)

Article 53

(8) No person shall be liable to any proceedings in any court in respect of anything said, or any vote given, by him when taking part in any proceedings of the Legislative Council or any committee thereof.

Republic of Bulgaria (1991)

Article 69

National representatives do not bear criminal responsibility for their expressed opinions or voting in the National Assembly.

Article 70

National representatives may not be detained, and criminal prosecution may not be initiated against them except for serious crimes and with the permission of the National Assembly or, when it is not in session, the Chairman of the National Assembly. No permission for detention is required when caught committing a serious crime, but in such a case, the National Assembly, or, when it is not in session, the Chairman of the National Assembly, is immediately notified.

Burkina Faso (1991)

Article 95

No Deputy can be pursued, investigated, arrested, detained or judged because of the opinions or votes made by him during the exercise of on the occasion of the exercise of his functions.

Article 96

Except in the case of flagrante delicto, any Deputy can only be pursued or arrested in a correctional or criminal matter with the authorization of at least one-third of the members of the Assembly during the sessions or of the Bureau of the Assembly outside of the sessions.

Burundi (1992)

Article 103

Parliamentarians may not be prosecuted, searched, arrested, detained or judged for opinions or votes issued during sessions.

During sessions, the deputies may be prosecuted only with the authorization of the Bureau of the National Assembly, except in case of flagrant offense.

When not in session, parliamentarians may be arrested only with the authorization of the Bureau of the National Assembly, except in case of flagrant offense, of previously authorized prosecution or definitive condemnation.

Cambodia (1993-1999)

Article 80

The deputies shall enjoy parliamentary immunity.

No assembly member shall be prosecuted, detained or arrested because of opinions expressed during the exercise of his (her) duties.

The accusation, arrest, or detention of an assembly member shall be made only with the permission of the National Assembly or by the Standing Committee of the

National Assembly between sessions, except in case of *flagrante delicto*. In that case, the competent authority shall immediately report to the National Assembly or to the Standing Committee for decision.

The decision made by the Standing Committee of the National Assembly shall be submitted to the National Assembly at its next session for approval by a $2/3$ majority vote of the assembly members.

In any case, detention or prosecution of a deputy shall be suspended by a $3/4$ majority vote of the National Assembly members.

Cameroon (1972-1996)

Article 14

(6) The conditions for the election of members of the National Assembly and of the Senate, as well as the immunities, ineligibilities, allowances and privileges of the members of Parliament shall be determined by law.

No further information available, however the Comparative Reference Compendium of the Inter-Parliamentary Union of 1986 suggests that the Members are inviolable.

Canada (1867-1982)

Article 18

The privileges, immunities, and powers to be held, enjoyed, and exercises by the Senate and by the House of Commons, and by the members thereof respectively, shall be such as are from time to time defined by Act of the Parliament of Canada, but so that any Act of the Parliament of Canada defining such privileges, immunities and powers shall not confer any privileges, immunities, or powers exceeding those at the passing of such Act held, enjoyed, and exercised by the Commons House of Parliament of the United Kingdom of Great Britain and Ireland, and by the members thereof.

Cape Verde (1981)

Article 181

(1) Deputies and Parliamentary Groups shall not have civil, criminal, or disciplinary liability for votes and opinions issued in the exercise of their duties.

(2) No Deputy may be detained or imprisoned without the authorization of the National Assembly, except in a case of flagrante delicto for a crime punishable by more than two years' imprisonment and, aside from flagrante delicto, for a crime punishable by more than eight years' imprisonment.

(3) Except in the case provided for in the second part of (2), at the beginning of a criminal procedure against a Deputy, the National Assembly shall decide whether the Deputy should be suspended during the trial.

Central African Republic (1994)

Article 49

The members of the National Assembly possess parliamentary immunity. In consequence, no Deputy may be pursued, investigated or arrested, detained or judged for reason of his opinions or votes emitted by him in the exercise of his functions.

No Deputy may, out of session, be arrested without the authorization of the Bureau of the National Assembly, except in the case of flagrant act, for authorized investigations or final sentences.

The investigation of a Deputy is suspended until the end of his mandate, except in the case of lifter parliamentary immunity, if the National Assembly requires it by an absolute majority vote.

Chad (1996)

Article 114

The members of Parliament enjoy parliamentary immunity.

No member of Parliament *[Parlementaire]* be prosecuted, sought, arrested, detained or judged for opinions or votes expressed by him in the exercise of his functions.

No member of Parliament may, during session, be prosecuted or arrested in a criminal or correctional matter without the authorization of the Assembly to which he belongs, except in the case of a flagrant offense.

No member of Parliament may, in between sessions, be arrested without the authorization of the Bureau of his Assembly, except in the case of a flagrant offense, of authorized prosecution or of definitive condemnation.

In case of crime or established offense, the immunity may be revoked by the Assembly to which the member of Parliament belongs during the sessions, or by the Bureau of the same Assembly between sessions.

In case of flagrant offense, the Bureau of the Assembly to which the member of Parliament belongs is notified immediately of the arrest.

Chile (2001)

Article 58

Deputies and Senators enjoy inviolability only with regard to the opinions they should express and the votes registered in performance of their duties in Congressional Sessions or in Committees.

No Deputy or Senator as of the date of his election of appointment or from the time of his incorporation into the respective Chamber may be tried or deprived of his freedom, except in the case of a flagrant crime, unless the Court of Appeals of the respective jurisdiction, in full court, has previously authorized the accusation, declaring that the process of law has been accepted. This decision may be appealed before the Supreme Court.

In case a Deputy or a Senator is arrested on charges of a flagrant crime, he shall be brought immediately before the respective Court of Appeals with the corresponding summary proceedings. The Court shall then proceed in accordance with the provisions of the aforementioned paragraph.

Upon declaration, by means of a final decision, that there are grounds for a process of law, the accused Deputy or Senator shall be suspended from his position and submitted to the competent judge.

Republic of China (1931-1982)

Article 74

No deputy to the National People's Congress may be arrested or placed on criminal trial without the consent of the presidium of the current session of the National People's Congress or, when the National People's Congress is not in session, without the consent of its Standing Committee.

Article 75

Deputies to the National People's Congress may not be called to legal account for their speeches or votes at its meetings.

Colombia (1991-1997)

Article 185

Congressmen will enjoy immunity for their opinions and the votes which they cast in the exercise of their office, without prejudice to the disciplinary rules included in the respective bylaws.

Article 186

For the crimes that congressmen commit, the Supreme Court of Justice is the sole authority that may order their detention. In case of 'flagrante delicto,' congressmen will have to be apprehended and placed immediately at the disposal of the same body.

Comoros (1992)

Article 33

While a session is in progress, no deputy may be prosecuted, searched, arrested, detained or judged without the authorization of the Federal Assembly, except in the case of flagrant offence or crime.

No deputy shall be prosecuted, searched, arrested, detained or judged because of his opinions or votes expressed in the exercise of his functions.

Congo (1992)

Article 101

No member of Parliament may be pursued, investigated, detained or judged for opinions or votes cast by him in the exercise of his functions. No deputy, no senator may, during the sessions, be arrested or pursued without the authorization of the bureau of the National Assembly, except in a case of a flagrant act (*délit*) of authorized pursuit or of definitive sentence (condemnation). No deputy, no senator may be pursued or arrested outside the session, without the authorization of the bureau of the chamber to which he belongs, except in the case of a flagrant act, authorized pursuits or definitive sentence.

Costa Rica (1949-1993)

Article 110

A deputy is not liable for opinions expressed in the Assembly. During its sessions he cannot be arrested on civil grounds, except by authorization of the Assembly or if the deputy consents thereto.

From the time he is declared elected as titular deputy or alternate, until his legal term expires, he may not be deprived of his liberty on penal grounds unless he has been previously suspended by the Assembly. Such immunity does not apply in case of *flagrante delicto* or if the deputy waives it. Nevertheless, a deputy who has been taken in *flagrante delicto* will be freed if the Assembly so orders.

Côte d'Ivoire (1960)

Article 67

No Deputy can be prosecuted, investigated, arrested, detained or judged on the occasion of his opinions or of the votes made by him in the exercise of his functions.

Article 68

During the term of the sessions, no member of Parliament can be prosecuted or arrested in a criminal or correctional matter without the authorization of the National Assembly, except in a case of *flagrante delicto*. No Deputy can, out of session, be arrested without the authorization of the Bureau of the National Assembly except in cases of *flagrante delicto*, authorized prosecutions or definitive condemnations. The detention or the prosecution of a member of Parliament is suspended if the National Assembly requires it.

Croatia (1990-2001)

Article 75

Members of the Croatian Sabor enjoy immunity. A member cannot be prosecuted, detained or punished for an opinion expressed or a vote cast in the Croatian Sabor.

A member cannot be detained, nor may criminal proceedings be instituted against him, without the consent of the Croatian Sabor.

A member may only be detained without the consent of the Croatian Sabor if he has been caught in the act of committing a criminal offence which carries a penalty of imprisonment of more than five years. In such a case, the President of the Croatian Sabor shall be notified.

When the Croatian Sabor is not in session, approval for the detention of a member, or for the continuation of criminal proceedings against him, shall be given and his right to immunity decided by the credentials-and-immunity committee of the Croatian Sabor.

Cuba (1992)

Article 83

No deputy to the National Assembly of People's Power may be arrested or place on trial without the authorization of the Assembly – or the Council of State if the Assembly is not in session – except in cases of flagrant offenses.

Cyprus (1960-1996)

Article 83

1. Representatives shall not be liable to civil or criminal proceedings in respect of any statement made or vote given by them in the House of Representatives.

2. A Representative cannot, without the leave of the High Court, be prosecuted, arrested or imprisoned so long as he continues to be a Representative. Such leave is not required in the case of an offence punishable with death or imprisonment for five years or more in case the offender is taken in the act. In such a case the High Court being notified forthwith by the competent authority decides whether it should grant or refuse leave for the continuation of the prosecution or detention so long as he continues to be a Representative.

3. If the High Court refuses to grant leave for the prosecution of a Representative, the period during which the Representative cannot thus be prosecuted shall not be reckoned for the purposes of any period of prescription for the offence in question.

4. If the High Court refuses to grant leave for the enforcement of a sentence of imprisonment imposed on a Representative by a competent court, the enforcement of such sentence shall be postponed until he ceases to be a Representative.

Czech Republic (1992)

Article 27

1. A deputy or senator may not be prosecuted because of his voting in the Chamber of Deputies or the Senate or their organs.

2. No criminal proceedings may be initiated against a deputy or senator because of speeches made in the Chamber of Deputies or the Senate or their organs. A deputy or senator is only subject to the disciplinary authority of the chamber of which he is a member.

3. A deputy or senator who is guilty of a misdemeanour is subject only to the disciplinary authority of the chamber of which he is a member, unless specified otherwise by law.

4. No criminal proceedings may be initiated against a deputy or senator without the consent of the chamber of which he is a member. If the chamber denies its consent, criminal proceedings are ruled our forever.

5. A deputy or senator may be detained only if he has been caught while committing a criminal offense or immediately thereafter. The appropriate authority is obliged to report the detainment without delay to the chairman of the chamber of which the detainee is a member; if the chamber's chairman does not give his consent within 24 hours after the detainee was handed over to the court, the appropriate authority is obliged to release him. At its first subsequent meeting the chamber shall decide with final validity on the admissibility of prosecution.

Denmark (1953)

Article 57

No Member of the Folketing shall be prosecuted or imprisoned in any manner whatsoever without the consent of Folketing, unless he is caught in flagrante delicto. Outside the Folketing no Member shall be held liable for his utterances in the Folketing save by the consent of the Folketing.

Dji Bouti (1977-1992)

Article 51

The members of the National Assembly shall enjoy parliamentary immunity.

No deputy may be prosecuted, sought, arrested, detained or tried as a result of the opinions or votes expressed by him in the exercise of his functions.

No deputy may, during sessions, be prosecuted or arrested for criminal or minor offences without the authorization of the National Assembly, except in the case of *flagrante delicto*. When the Assembly is not in session, no deputy may be arrested without the authorization of the Secretariat of the National Assembly except in the case of *flagrante delicto*, of authorized prosecution or final conviction.

The detention or prosecution of a deputy shall be suspended if the National Assembly so requires.

Republic of Dominica (1978-1984)

Article 43

Without prejudice to any provision made by Parliament relating to the powers, privileges and immunities of the House and its committees, or the privileges and immunities of the members and officers of the House and of other persons concerned in the business of the House or its committees, no civil or criminal proceedings may be instituted against any member of the House for words spoken before, or written in a report to, the House of a committee thereof or by reason of any matter or thing brought by him therein by petition, bill, resolution, motion or otherwise.

Dominican Republic

Article 31

The members of both Chambers shall enjoy the fullest penal immunity for the opinions they express in sessions.

Article 32

No Senator or Deputy may be deprived of his freedom during the legislative session without the authorization of the Chamber to which he belongs, except in the case of his being apprehended in the moment of committing a crime. In all cases the Senate or Chamber of Deputies, or, if they are not in session or there is not quorum, any member, may demand that a member who has been detained, arrested, imprisoned, or in any other way deprived of his liberty, be set free for the duration of the legislative session or any portion thereof. To this end, the President of the Senate or of the Chamber of Deputies, or the Senator or Deputy, as the case may be, shall make such request to the Attorney General *[Procurador General]* of the Republic; and if necessary, shall give the order for liberation directly, for which he may request the assistance of the public force, which must be given to him by every depositary thereof.

East Timor (2002)

Article 94

1. The Members are not responsible for civil, criminal or disciplinary matters in regard to votes and opinions expressed by them while performing their functions.
2. Parliamentary immunities may be withdrawn in accordance with the Rules of Procedure of the National Parliament.

Ecuador (1998)

Article 137

Deputies are not civilly or penally responsible for the votes and opinions they emit in the exercise of their functions.

Criminal charges cannot be initiated against then without the previous authorization of the National Congress, nor will they be deprived of their liberty, except in cases of flagrante delicto. If the petition of a competent judge for authorization to make a judgment is not contested within a period of thirty days it will be understood as granted. The passing of the aforementioned period is suspended during recesses. Criminal trials initiated before the post is occupied shall continue to be heard before the competent judge.

Egypt (1971)

Article 98

Members of the People's Assembly shall not be censured for any opinions or thoughts expressed by them in the performance of their tasks in the Assembly or its committees.

Article 99

No member of the People's Assembly shall be subject to a criminal prosecution without the permission of the Assembly except in cases of *flagrante delicto*.

If the Assembly is not in session, the permission of the President of the Assembly must be taken.

The Assembly must be notified of the measures taken in its first subsequent session.

El Salvador (1983-1996)

Article 125

The Deputies represent the whole nation *[pueblo]* and are not bound by any imperative mandate. They are inviolable and shall not have responsibility at any time for the opinions or votes they emit.

Equatorial Guinea (1990-1993)

Article 68

No representative may be prosecuted or detained for opinions expressed during and after the exercise of his duties in the Chamber.

No jurisdiction may detain or prosecute a Representative in the Chamber without the prior permission of the Executive Board of the Chamber, except in case of flagrante delicto.

Eritrea

Article 38

2. No member of the National Assembly may be charged for any crime, unless he be apprehended in flagrante delicto. However, where it is deemed necessary to lift his immunity, such a member may be charged in accordance with procedures determined by the National Assembly.

3. No member of the National Assembly may be charged or otherwise by answerable for statements made of submitted by him at any meeting of the National Assembly or any meeting of its committees or any utterance or statement made outside the National Assembly in connection with is duty as member thereof.

4. The duties, responsibilities, immunities and compensation of the members of the National Assembly shall be determined by law; and all members shall be entitles to the protection of such immunities.

Estonia (1992)

Article 76

Every member of the *Riigikogu* shall enjoy immunity. A member of the *Riigikogu* may be charged with a criminal offence only on proposal by the Legal Chancellor and with the consent of the majority of the members of the *Riigikogu*.

Ethiopia (1995)

Article 63

1. No member of the House of the Federation may be prosecuted on account of any vote he casts or opinion he expresses in the House, not shall any administrative action be taken against any member on such grounds.

2. No member of the House of the Federation may be arrested or prosecuted without the permission of the House except in the case of flagrante delicto.

Fiji Islands (1990-1997)

Article 74

(2) The Parliament may prescribe the powers, privileges and immunities of the Houses of the Parliament.

(5) Each House of Parliament may make rules and orders with respect to:
   (a) the way in which its powers, privileges and immunities may be exercised and upheld [.]

Chapter 5, Parliamentary Powers and Privileges, 1978

Immunity from legal proceedings

3. No civil or criminal proceedings may be instituted against any member for words spoken before, or written in a report to, either House of Parliament or to a committee thereof, or by reason of any matter or thing to brought by him by petition, Bill, motion or otherwise.

Freedom from arrest

4. No member shall be liable to arrest –
   (a) for any civil debt whilst going to, attending at or returning from a sitting of either House of Parliament or any committee thereof;

(b) within the precincts of Parliament while either House of Parliament or a committee is sitting, for any criminal offence without the consent of the Speaker or the President, as may be appropriate.

Finland (1999)

Section 30

A Representative shall not be prevented from carrying out his or her duties as a Representative.

A Representative shall not be charged in a court of law nor be deprived of liberty owing to opinions expressed by the Representative in the Parliament or owing to conduct in the consideration of a matter, unless the Parliament has consented to the same by a decision supported by at least five sixths of the votes cast.

If a Representative has been arrested or detained, the Speaker of the Parliament shall be immediately notified of this. A Representative shall not be arrested or detained before the commencement of a trial without the consent of the Parliament, unless he or she is for substantial reasons suspected of having committed a crime for which the minimum punishment is imprisonment for at least six months.

Section 31

Each Representative has the right to speak freely in the Parliament on all matters under consideration and on how they are dealt with.

France (1789-2003)

Article 26

No member of Parliament can be prosecuted, sought, arrested, detained or tried because of opinions expressed, or votes cast in the exercise of their functions.

No member of Parliament can be subject (*objets*) in a criminal or correctional matter, of an arrest or of any other measure [which] deprives or restricts liberty, except with the authorization of the Bureau of the Assembly of which he [she] is a member. The authorization is not required, in case of a crime or misdemeanor of final conviction (*condemnation définitive*).

The detention, the measure which deprive or restrict the liberty or the prosecution of a member of Parliament are suspended for the duration if the session of the Assembly, of which he [she] is a part, so requests.

Gabon (1991-1997)

Article 38

No member of the Parliament may be prosecuted, investigated, arrested, detained or judged as a result of the opinions of votes he expressed in the exercise of his functions.

Any member of Parliament may, during sessions, only be prosecuted, investigated, arrested for a criminal, correctional or simple police matter, with the authorization of the Bureau of the concerned Chamber, except in the case of flagrant offense or definitive condemnation.

The detention or the prosecution of a member of Parliament will be suspended until the end of his mandate, except in the case of a waiver of parliamentary immunity.

The Gambia (1996)

Article 113

There shall be freedom of speech and debate in the National Assembly and that freedom shall not be impeached or questioned in any court or place outside the National Assembly.

Article 114

Without prejudice to the generality of *section 113*, no civil or criminal proceedings shall be instituted against a member of the National Assembly in any court or other place outside the National Assembly by reason of anything said by him.

Georgia (1995-2003)

Article 52

2. The bringing of a Member of Parliament to criminal responsibility, his detention or arrest, the search of his place of residence, car, place of work, as well as a personal search is permitted only with the consent of the Parliament. Arrest at the scene of a crime constitutes an exception, about which Parliament is immediately notified. In this case, if Parliament does not give its consent, the detained or arrested member of Parliament must be immediately released.

4. A Member of Parliament does not suffer criminal responsibility for his ideas and opinions expressed by him in fulfillment of his obligations in Parliament or outside its bounds.

Germany (1949)

Article 46

(1) At no time may a Member be subjected to court proceedings for disciplinary action or otherwise called to account outside the Bundestag for vote cast or for any speech or debate in the Bundestag or in any of its committees. This provision does not apply to defamatory insults.

(2) A Member may not be called to account or arrested for a punishable offense without permission of the Bundestag, unless he is apprehended while committing the offense or in the course of the following day.

(3) The permission of the Bundestag is also required for any other restriction of a Member's freedom of the person or for the initiation of proceedings against a Member under Article 18.

(4) Any criminal proceedings or any proceedings under Article 18 against a Member and any detention or other restriction of the freedom of the person shall be suspended at the demand of the Bundestag.

Ghana (1992-1996)

Article 115

There shall be freedom of speech, debate and proceedings in Parliament and that freedom shall not be impeached or questioned in any court or place out of Parliament.

Article 116

(1) Subject to the provisions of this article, but without prejudice to the general effect of article 115 of this Constitution, civil or criminal proceedings shall not be instituted against a member of Parliament in any court or place out of Parliament for any matter or thing brought by him in or before Parliament by petition, bill, motion or otherwise.

Greece (1975)

Article 60

1. Members of Parliament enjoy unrestricted freedom of opinions and right to vote according to their conscience.

Article 61

2. A Member of Parliament may be prosecuted only for libel, according to the law, after leave has been granted by Parliament. The Court of Appeals shall be competent to hear the case. Such leave is deemed to be conclusively denied if Parliament does not decide within forty-five days from the date the charges have been submitted to the Speaker. In case of refusal to grant leave or if the time-limit lapses without action, no charge can be brought for the act committed by the Member of Parliament. This paragraph shall be applicable as of the next parliamentary session.

Article 62

During the parliamentary term the Members of Parliament shall not be prosecuted, arrested, imprisoned or otherwise confined without prior leave granted by Parliament. Likewise, a member of a dissolved Parliament shall not be prosecuted for political crimes during the period between the dissolution of Parliament and the declaration of the election of the members of the new Parliament. Leave shall be deemed not granted if Parliament does not decide within three months of the date the request for prosecution by the public prosecutor was transmitted to the Speaker.

The three month limit is suspended during the Parliament's recess.

No leave is required when Members of Parliament are caught in the act of committing a felony.

Grenada (1983-1989)

Article 50

(2) Parliament may, for the purpose of the orderly and effective discharge of the business of the Senate and the House of Representatives, make provision for the powers, privileges and immunities of those Houses and the committees and the members thereof.

No further information is available.

Guatemala (1985)

Article 161

Deputies are representatives of the people and dignitaries of the Nation; as a guarantee for the exercise of their functions they will enjoy, from the day they are declared elected, the following prerogatives:

a. Personal immunity from arrest or trial if the Supreme Court of Justice does not previously declare that there is probable cause, after examining the report of the investigating judge that will be named for this end. The case of flagrante delicto is excepted, for which that deputy shall be immediately place at the disposition of the Directive Board of the Permanent Commission of the Congress for the purpose of the corresponding initial judgement.

b. They cannot be held responsible for their opinions, initiative, and the manner of handling public business in the performance of their work *[cargo]*. All the dependencies of the State have the obligation to show deputies the consideration attaching to their high position. These prerogatives do not authorize arbitrariness, excess of personal initiative, or any type of action tending to undermine the principle of no reelection for the exercise of the Presidency of the Republic. Only the Congress will be competent to judge and determine if there has been arbitrariness or excess and to impose the appropriate disciplinary sanctions. Considering the declaration to which paragraph (a) in this article refers, those accused are subject to the jurisdiction of the competent judge. If he should decree provisional imprisonment for them, they shall be suspended from their functions as long as the incarceration decree is not revoked. In the case of firm condemnatory sentence, it shall remain vacant.

Guinea (1990)

Article 52

No member of the National Assembly shall be prosecuted, investigated, arrested, detained or tried because of opinions or votes expressed by him while exercising his functions as Deputy.

No deputy shall be prosecuted or arrested on penal grounds while the National Assembly is in session except with the Assembly's authorization, except in the case of *flagrante delicto*.

No deputy can be arrested or detained while the Assembly is not in session without the authorization of the office of the National Assembly except in the case of *flagrante delicto*, prosecutions authorized by the Assembly or final condemnations.

The preventative detention or prosecution of a Deputy shall be suspended if the Assembly requires it.

Guinea – Bissau (1991)

Article 53

1. No deputy may be disturbed, prosecuted, arrested, imprisoned, judged, or condemned for his voting record or the opinions he expressed while performing his duties as Deputy.

2. Except if apprehended in the act of committing an offense [flagrante delicto] that bears a penalty equal to or greater than two years of forced labor, or with the previous consent of the National Popular Assembly or the Council of State, Deputies may not be prosecuted or imprisoned for a criminal or disciplinary questioned, whether judged or not.

Article 54

1. The rights and privileges, as well as the powers and duties of Deputies, shall be regulated by law.

Guyana (1980-1995)

Article 172

(1) Subject to the provisions of paragraphs (2), (3) and (4), Parliament may by law determine the privileges, immunities and powers of the National Assembly and the members thereof.

(2) No civil or criminal proceedings may be instituted against any member of the Assembly or to a committee thereof or by reason of any matter or thing brought by him therein by petition, bill, resolution, motion or otherwise.

(3) For the duration of any session, members of the Assembly shall enjoy freedom from arrest for any civil debt.

Haiti (1984-1987)

Article 114

Members of the Legislature are inviolable from the day they take oath up to the expiration of their term, subject to the provisions or Article 115 below.

Article 114-1

They may at no time be prosecuted or attacked for the opinions and votes cast by them in the discharge of their duties.

Article 114-2

No member of the Legislature shall be subject to civil imprisonment during his term of office.

Article 115

No member of the Legislature may during his term be arrested under ordinary law for a crime, a minor offense or a petty violation, except by authorization of the House of which he is a member, unless he is apprehended in the act of committing an offense punishable by death, personal restraint or penal servitude or the loss of civil rights. In that case, the matter is referred to the House of Deputies or the Senate without delay if the Legislature is in session, and if not, if shall be taken up at the next regular or special session.

Honduras

Article 200

Beginning on the day they are declared elected, deputies shall be entitled to the following prerogatives:

1. Personal immunity against the search of their person or their home, being arrested, accused, or tried, even during a state of siege, unless the National Congress has not previously declared that there is probable cause for a trial;

3. Not to be responsible at any time for their initiatives of Law nor for their opinions expressed during their term of office;

4. Exemption from civil suit during the period covered by fifteen days before and fifteen days after a ordinary or extraordinary session of Congress, except as to counterclaims.

Hungary (1949)

Article 20

(3) Members of parliament are entitled to immunity as defined and regulated in the law on their legal status.

Act LV of 1990
On the Legal Status of Members of Parliament
Chapter II
Parliamentary Immunity of MPs

Section 4

Active or former MPs can not be accountable before court, or by any other authority, for their votes cast, or facts and opinions stated in the course of the duration of their mandate. This immunity shall not be applicable in case of violation of state secret, of defamation or libel, and in connection with the accountability of MPs under civil law.

Section 5

(1) MPs can be only arrested in case of flagrante delicto. Criminal procedures or legal procedures for petty offences against MPs can only be started and pursued with prior permission given by Parliament. Prior permission by Parliament is also required for law enforcement actions against MPs in criminal procedures. (This is followed by the immunity waiving process in subsections (2) to (7).)

Iceland (1944-1995)

Article 49

No Member of Althingi may be subjected to custody on remand during a session of Althingi without the permission of Althingi, nor may a criminal action be brought against him unless he is caught in the act of committing a crime. No Member of Althingi may be made responsible outside Althingi for statements made by him in Althingi, except with the permission of Althingi.

India (1950-2002)

Article 105

(1) Subject to the provisions of this Constitution and to the rules and standing orders regulating the procedure of Parliament, there shall be freedom of speech in Parliament.

(2) No member of Parliament shall be liable to any proceedings in any court in respect of anything said or any vote given by him in Parliament or any committee thereof, and no person shall be so liable in respect of the publication by or under the authority of either House of Parliament of any report, paper, votes or proceedings.

(3) In other respects, the powers, privileges and immunities of each House of Parliament, and of the members and the committees of each House, shall be such as may from time to time be defined by Parliament by law, and, until so defined, [89][shall be those of that House and of its members and committees immediately before the coming into force of section 15 of the Constitution (Forty-fourth Amendment) Act, 1978].

(4) The provisions of clauses (1), (2) and (3) shall apply in relation to persons who by virtue of this Constitution have the right to speak in, and otherwise to take part in the proceedings of, a House of Parliament or any committee thereof as they apply in relation to members of Parliament.

Indonesia (1945)

Unofficial Translation
ACT No. 23/2003
Article 38 – Immunity Privileges

- A member of MPR (People's Consultative Assembly), DPR (House of Representatives), DPD (Regional Representatives), DPRD Provinsi (Provincial House of Representatives), or DPRD Kabupaten/Kota (Regency/Municipal People's Representatives) cannot be prosecuted in the court of law for his/her verbal or written statements, inquiries and/or opinions set forth in MPR, DPR, DPRD Provinsi and DPRD Kabupaten/Kota sessions, as long as they do not violate the code of conduct and code of ethics of each institution.

- The stipulation of paragraph (1) does not apply if a member discloses any information deemed confidential under closed parliamentary meetings or under stipulations of Criminal Code, Book II, Chapter I regarding disclosure of national's secrets.

- A member of MPR, DPR, DPD, DPRD Provinsi, or DPRD Kabupaten/Kota cannot be dismissed for his/her verbal or written statements, inquiries and/or opinions set forth in MPR, DPR, DPRD Provinsi and DPRD Kabupaten/Kota sessions.

Article 106 – Investigation

1. If a member of MPR, DPR, or DPD is under suspicion of criminal activities, a written approval from the President must be obtained for the summon, request for information, and investigation of this member.

2. If a member of DPRD Provinsi is under suspicion of criminal activities, a written approval from the Minister of Internal Affairs on behalf of the President must be obtained for the summon, request for information, and investigation of this member.

3. If a member of DPRD Kabupaten/Kota is under suspicion of criminal activities, a written approval from the Governor of behalf of the Minister of International

Affairs must be obtained for the summon, request for information, and investigation of this member.

4. The Stipulation of paragraph (1), (2), and (3) do not apply if a member of MPR, DPR, DPD, DPRD Provinsi, or DPRD Kabupaten/Kota commits corruption, terrorism act or is caught in the act of criminal activities.

5. In the event of the implementation of paragraph (4), the investigation must be reported to the relevant authority in order to obtain his/her approval within 48 hours (at the latest).

Iran (1979-1992)

Article 86

Members of the Assembly are completely free in expressing their views and casting their votes in the course of performing their duties as representatives, and they cannot be prosecuted or arrested for opinions expressed in the Assembly or votes cast in the course of performing their duties as representatives.

Iraq (2004)

Article 34

Each member of the National Assembly shall enjoy immunity for statements made while the Assembly is in session, and the member may not be sued before the courts for such. A member may not be placed under arrest during a session of the National Assembly, unless the member is accused of a crime and the National Assembly agrees to lift his immunity or if he is caught *in flagrante delicto* in the commission of a felony.

Ireland (1937-2002)

Article 10

Each House shall make its own rules and standing orders, with power to attach penalties for their infringement, and shall have power to ensure freedom of debate, to protect its official documents and the private papers of its members, and to protect itself and its members against any person or persons interfering with, molesting or attempting to corrupt its members in the exercise of their duties.

Article 12

All official reports and publications of the Oireachtas or of either House thereof and utterances made in either House wherever published shall be privileged.

Article 13

The members of each House of the Oireachtas shall, except in case of treason as defined in this Constitution, felony or breach of the peach, be privileged from arrest in going to and returning from, and while within the precincts of, either House, and shall not, in respect of any utterance in either House, be amenable to any court or any authority other than the House itself.

Israel (1951)

Article 62

(a) A Member of the Knesset shall bear no civil or criminal liability in respect of a vote or an oral or written expression of opinion, if such vote or opinions be given in the carrying out of his mandate as a Member of the Knesset.

(b) A Member of the Knesset shall not be arrested unless caught while committing a felony. The authority which has arrested a Member of the Knesset shall immediately verify such fact to the Chairman of the Knesset. A Member o the Knesset who has been arrested shall not be kept under arrest for more than ten days except with the approval of the Knesset or of a Committee of the Knesset authorised by the Knesset thereto.

(c) A Member of the Knesset shall be immune from a search of his person, his premises or his belongings.

(e) The immunity of a Member of the Knesset under subsections (a) and (d) shall continue when he has ceased to be a Member of the Knesset.

(f) Matters for exclusion from the scope of the immunity under these sections may be prescribed by law.

Italy (1944)

Article 68

The members of Parliament may not be made to answer for opinions expressed or votes given in the exercise of their functions.

Without the authorization of the Chamber to which he belongs, no member of Parliament may be subjected to search of his person or domicile, nor may he be arrested or otherwise deprived of his personal freedom, or held in detention, save [in the case of] the execution of a final [irrevocable] sentence of convictions, or if he be caught in the act of committing an offense, *in flagrante*, for which arrest is mandatory.

An analogous authorization is required [in order to] subject members of Parliament to the interception, in any form, of [their] conversations or communications or to the sequestering of [their] correspondence.

Jamaica (1962-1983)

Article 48

(1) Subject to the provisions of this Constitution, Parliament may make laws for the peace, order and good government of Jamaica.

(3) Without prejudice to the generality of subsection (1) and subject to the provisions of subsections (3), (4) and (5) of this section Parliament may be law determine the privileges, immunities and powers of the two Houses and the members thereof.

(4) No civil or criminal proceedings may be instituted against any member of either House for words spoken before, or written in a report to, the House of which he is a member or to a committee thereof or to any join committee of both Houses of by reason of any matter or thing brought by him therein by petition, bill, resolution, motion or otherwise.

(5) For the duration of any session members of both Houses shall enjoy freedom from arrest for any civil debt except a debt the contraction of which constitutes a criminal offence.

(6) No process issued by any court in the exercise of its civil jurisdiction shall be served or executed within the precincts of either House while such House is sitting or through the President or the Speaker, the Clerk or any officer of either House.

Japan (1946)

Article 50

Except in cases provided by law, members of both Houses shall be exempt from apprehension while the Diet is in session, and any members apprehended before the opening of the session shall be freed during the term of the session upon demand of the House.

Article 51

Members of both Houses shall not be held liable outside the House for speeches, debates of votes cast inside the House.

Jordan (1971-1984)

Article 86

(i) No Senator or Deputy shall be detained or tried during the holding of the sessions of the National Assembly unless the Senate or the House of Deputies, as the case may be, decide by a majority resolution, that there is sufficient reason for his detention or trial or unless he was arrested in the course of committing a criminal offence. In the event of his arrest in this manner, the Senate or the House of Deputies, must be notified immediately.

(ii) If a member is detained, for any reason, while the National Assembly is not sitting, the Prime Minister shall notify the Senate or the House of Deputies when it reassembles, of the proceedings which were taken against him, coupled with the necessary explanation.

Article 87

Every Senator or Deputy shall have complete freedom of speech and expression of opinion within the limits of the Standing Orders of the Senate of House of Deputies, as the case may be, and shall not be answerable in respect of any vote he gave or opinion expressed, or speech made, by him during the meetings of the House.

Kenya (1969-1997)

Article 57

Without prejudice to the powers conferred by section 56, Parliament may, for the purpose of the orderly and effective discharge of the business of the National Assembly, provide for the powers, privileges and immunities of the Assembly and its committees and members.

National Assembly (Powers and Privileges) Act 1980, Chapter 6

4. No civil or criminal proceedings shall be instituted against any member for words spoken before, or written in a report to, the Assembly or a committee, or by reason of any matter or thing brought by him therein by petition, Bill, resolution, motion or otherwise.

5. No member shall be liable to arrest for any civil debt except a debt the contraction of which constitutes a criminal offence, whilst going to, attending at or returning from a sitting or the Assembly or any committee.

Kiribati (1979-1995)

Article 76

(2) No civil or criminal proceedings may be instituted against any member of the Maneaba for words spoken before, or written in a report to, the Maneaba or a committee of the Maneaba, or by reason of any matter or thing brought by him in the Maneaba or in a committee of the Maneaba.

Democratic People's Republic of Korea (1972-1998)

Article 99

Deputies to the Supreme People's Assembly are guaranteed inviolability as such.

No deputy to the Supreme People's Assembly can be arrested or punished without the consent of the Supreme People's Assembly or, when it is not in session, without the consent of its Standing Committee.

Republic of Korea (1980-1987)

Article 44

(1) During the sessions of the National Assembly, no member of the National Assembly shall be arrested or detained without the consent of the National Assembly except in case of *flagrante delicto*.

(2) In case of apprehension or detention of a member of the National Assembly prior to the opening of a session, such member shall be released during the session upon the request of the National Assembly, except in case of *flagrante delicto*.

Article 45

No member of the National Assembly shall be held responsible outside the National Assembly for opinions officially expressed or votes cast in the Assembly.

Kuwait (1971)

Article 110

A member of the National Assembly shall be free to express any views of opinions in the Assembly or in its committees. Under no circumstances shall he be held liable in respect thereof.

Article 111

Except in cases of flagrante delicto, no measure of inquiry, search, arrest, detention or any other penal measure may be taken against a member while the Assembly is in session, except with the authorisation of the Assembly. The Assembly shall be notified of any penal measure that may be taken during its session in accordance with the foregoing provision. The Assembly shall always at its first meeting be notified or any such measure taken against any of its members while it was not sitting. In all cases, if the Assembly does not give a decision regarding a request for authorisation within one month from the date of its receipt, permission shall be deemed to have been given.

Kyrgyz Republic (1993-2003)

Article 56

4. A Deputy of the Jogorku Kenesh of the Kyrgyz Republic enjoys the right to immunity. He cannot be subjected to persecution for opinions expressed in connections with the activity of a Deputy or for the results of voting in the Jogorku Kenesh of the Kyrgyz Republic. A Deputy may not be detained or arrested, subjected to search or body search, except for cases when caught at a crime scene. Bringing a Deputy to a criminal as well as administrative responsibility imposed according to a court procedure is only permitted with the consent of the Jogorku Kenesh of the Kyrgyz Republic.

Laos (1991)

Article 51

Members of the National Assembly shall not be prosecuted in court of detained without the approval of the National Assembly of the National Assembly Standing Committee during the two sessions of the National Assembly.

In cases involving gross and urgent offenses, the organisations detaining members of the National Assembly must immediately report to the National Assembly or to the National Assembly Standing Committee during the two sessions of the National Assembly for consideration and decisions concerning them. Inquiries and interrogations shall not cause the absence of prosecuted members from the National Assembly session.

Latvia (1922-1998)

Article 28

The members of the Saeima shall be exempt from judicial, administrative and disciplinary prosecution, in connection with their voting and with ideas expressed in the fulfillment of their duties. Even if it is done through the fulfillment of official duties, members of the Saeima are liable to prosecution for:

1) the dissemination of defamatory information with the knowledge that it is false; or

2) the dissemination of defamatory information about private or family life.

Article 29

Members of the Saeima may not be arrested or searched, nor may their personal liberty be restricted in any way, without the sanction of the Saeima. Members of the Saeima shall be liable to arrest, if apprehended in the act of committing a crime. The Board of the Saeima shall be notified of the arrest of any member of the Saeima within twenty-four hours. A report shall be presented by the Board at the next sitting of the Saeima, whereupon the Saeima shall decide as to whether the member shall remain under arrest or be liberated. During the period between sessions, the Board of the Saeima shall determine whether the member of the Saeima shall remain under arrest.

Article 30

Members of the Saeima shall not be subject to any criminal prosecution or administrative punishment without the sanction given by the Saeima.

Lebanon (1926-1995)

Article 39

No member of the Chamber may be prosecuted because of the opinions and ideas he expresses during the term of his representation.

Article 40

No Chamber member may be prosecuted or arrested, during the session, for committing a crime, unless authorized by the Chamber, except in case he is caught in the act.

Lesotho (1993)

Article 81

(3) Parliament may, for the purpose of the orderly and effective discharge of the business of the two Houses, make provision for the powers, privileges and immunities of those Houses and the Committees and the members thereof (including any person who is President or Vice-President or Speaker or Deputy Speaker of either House, having been elected from among persons who were not members thereof).

No further information is available.

Liberia (1847)

Article 42

No member of the Senate or House of Representatives shall be arrested, detained, prosecuted or tried as a result of opinions expressed or votes cast in the exercise of the functions of his office. Members shall be privileged from arrest while attending, going to or returning from sessions of the Legislature, except for treason, felony or breach of the peace. All official acts done or performed and all statements made in the Chambers of the Legislature shall be privileged, and no Legislator shall be held accountable or punished therefor.

Libya

No Constitution since the overthrow of King Idris in 1969

Liechtenstein (1921-1981)

Article 56

No representative may be arrested while the Diet is in session without the assent of that body, unless he is apprehended in flagrante delicto.

In the latter case, the arrest and the grounds therefore must be notified forthwith to the Diet, which shall decide whether the arrest is to be sustained. All papers relating to the case must be placed immediately at the disposal of the Diet if it so requests.

If a representative is arrested at a time when the Diet is not in session, the National Committee must be notified forthwith, and informed at the same time of the grounds for the arrest.

Lithuania (1991)

Article 62

The person of a Seimas member shall be inviolable.

Seimas members may not be found criminally responsible, may not be arrested, and may not be subjected to any other restriction of personal freedom without the consent of the Seimas.

Seimas members may not be persecuted for voting or speeches in the Seimas. However, legal actions may be instituted against Seimas members according the general procedure if they are guilty of personal insult or slander.

Luxembourg (1968)

Article 68

No Deputy can be prosecuted or tried on account of opinions expressed or votes cast by him in the course of his duties.

Article 69

No Deputy can be prosecuted or arrested in a repressive matter in the course of a session, without the Chamber's authorization, unless he is caught in the act. – None of its members may be imprisoned during the session without the same authorization. – The detention or prosecution of a Deputy is suspended during and throughout session if the Chamber so demands.

Macedonia (1991)

Article 64

Representatives enjoy immunity.

A Representative cannot be held to have committed a criminal offence or be detained owing to views he/she has expressed or to the way he/she has voted in the Assembly.

A Representative cannot be detained without the approval of the Assembly unless found committing a criminal offence for which a prison sentence of at least five years is prescribed.

The Assembly can decide to invoke immunity for a Representative without his/her request, should it be necessary for the performance of the Representative's office.

Madagascar (1998)

Article 69

No Deputy may be prosecuted, investigated, arrested, detained or judged on the occasion of the opinions or votes expressed by him in the exercise of his functions. No Deputy may, during legislative sessions, be prosecuted or arrested, in a criminal or correctional matter, without the authorization of the Assembly, except in the case of flagrante delicto.

No Deputy may, outside of sessions, be arrested without the authorization of the Bureau of the Assembly, except in the case of flagrante delicto, authorized prosecutions or definitive condemnation.

Article 81

The provisions of Articles 67 to 75 are applicable to the Senate.

Malawi (1994)

Article 60

(1) The Speaker, every Deputy Speaker, every member of the National Assembly and every member of the Senate shall, except in cases of treason, be privileged from arrest while going to, returning from, or while in the precincts of the National Assembly or the Senate, and shall not, in respect of any utterance that forms part of the proceedings in the National Assembly or the Senate, be amenable to any other action or proceedings in any court, tribunal or body other than Parliament.

Article 10

(1) Subject to Clauses (2), (3) and (4)

  (a) every citizen has the right to freedom of speech and expression;

(2) Parliament may by law impose –

  (a) on the rights conferred by paragraph (a) of Clause (1), such restrictions as it deems necessary or expedient in the interest of the security of the Federation or any part thereof, friendly relations with other countries, public order or morality and restrictions designed to protect the privileges of Parliament or of any Legislative Assembly or to proved against contempt of court, defamation, or any incitement to any offence [.]

(4) In imposing restrictions in the interest of the security of the Federation or any part thereof or public order under Clause (2) (a), Parliament may pass law prohibiting the questioning of any matter, right, status, position, privilege, sovereignty or prerogative established or protected by the provisions of Part III, Article 152, 153 or 181 otherwise than in relation to the implementation thereof as may be specified in such law.

Article 63

(2)No person shall be liable to any proceedings in any court in respect of anything said or any vote given by him when taking part in any proceedings of either House of Parliament or any committee thereof.

(4) Clause (2) shall not apply to any person charged with an offence under the law passed by Parliament under Clause (4) of Article 10 or with an offense under the Sedition Act 1948 as amended by the Emergency (Essential Powers) Ordinance No. 45, 1970.

(5) Notwithstanding Clause (4), no person shall be liable to any proceedings in any court in respect of anything said by him of the Yang di-Pertuan Agong or a Ruler when taking part in any proceedings of either House or Parliament or any committee thereof except where he advocates the abolition of the constitutional position of the Yang di-Pertuan Agong

as the Supreme Head of the Federation or the constitutional position of the Ruler of a State, as the case may be.

Maldives (1998)

Article 84

No member of the People's Majlis shall be held liable in respect of any thought expressed or anything said without contradicting the basic tenets of Islam or any vote given by him in a duly constituted sitting of the People's Majlis or any committee thereof.

Mali (1992)

Article 62

No member of the National Assembly may be prosecuted, sought, arrested, detained, or judged because of his opinions or votes expressed by him in the exercise of his functions.

No member of the National Assembly can, during its sessions, be prosecuted or arrested for criminal or correctional offenses without the authorization of the National Assembly, except in the case of a flagrant offense.

No member of the National Assembly may, out of session, be arrested without the authorization of the Bureau of the National Assembly, except in the case of flagrant offense, or authorized prosecutions or of definitive condemnation.

The detention or the prosecution of a member of the National Assembly is suspended if the National Assembly so requests.

Malta (1964-2001)

Article 65

(1) Subject to the provisions of this Constitution, Parliament may make laws for the peace, order and good government of Malta.

(2) Without prejudice to the generality of sub-article (1) and subject to the provisions of sub-articles (3), (4) and (5) or this article, Parliament may be law determine the privileges, immunities and powers of the House of Representatives and the members thereof.

(3) No civil or criminal proceedings may be instituted against any member of the House of Representatives for words spoken before, or written in a report to, the House or a committee thereof or by reason of any matter or thing brought by him therein by petition, bill, resolution, motion or otherwise.

(4) For the duration of any session members of the House of Representatives shall enjoy freedom from arrest for any civil debt except a debt the contraction of which constitutes a criminal offence.

(5) No process issued by any court in the exercise of its civil jurisdiction shall be served or executed within the precincts of the House of Representatives while the House is sitting or through the Speaker, the Clerk or any officer of the House.

Marshall Islands (1979-1995)

Section 16

Privileges of the Nitijela and its Members

(2) Members of the Nitijela shall, except in cases of felony, be privileged from arrest during any session of the Nitijela, and in going to or returning from the same.

(3) Neither the Speaker not any officer of the Nitijela in whom powers are vested for the regulation of procedure or the conduct of business or the maintenance of order shall, in relation to the exercise of any of those in powers,

be subject to the jurisdiction of any court; but this shall not be taken to preclude the exercise of judicial power under Section 7 of Article II or judicial review, in an action against the Clerk of the Nitijela as nominal defendant, pursuant to Section 9 of this Article.

(4) Neither the Nitijela nor any member of the Nitijela shall be subject to any proceedings outside that body, or subjected to any liability, civil or criminal, in relation to the casting of any vote, the making of any statement, the publication of any document or the taking of any other action as part of the official business of the Nitijela.

Mauritania (1991)

Article 50

No member of Parliament may be prosecuted, pursued, arrested, detained or tried because of the opinions or votes voiced by him during the exercise of his functions. No member of Parliament, while Parliament is in session, may be prosecuted or arrested for a criminal or penal matter, except with the authorization of the assembly to which he belongs, unless it is a case of *flagrante delicto*.

No member of Parliament, while Parliament is out of session, may be arrested, except with the authorization of the office of the assembly to which he belongs, unless it is a case of *flagrante delicto*, or authorized prosecution or a judicial sentence.

The detention or prosecution of a member of Parliament shall be suspended if the assembly to which he belongs demands it.

Mauritius (1968-1997)

Article 45

(2) Without prejudice to subsection (1), Parliament may by law determine the privileges, immunities and powers of the Assembly and its members.

Article 3 (National Assembly (Privileges, Immunities and Powers), July 1992)
Immunity from legal proceedings

No civil or criminal proceedings may be instituted against the Speaker or any member for words spoken before, or written in a report to, the Assembly or any committee, or by reason of any matter or thing brought by him in the Assembly by petition, Bill, resolution, motion or otherwise.

Mexico (1857-2003)

Article 61

Deputies and Senators are inviolable for opinions expressed by them in the discharge of their offices and shall never be called to account for them.

The president of each Chamber shall safeguard the respect for the constitutional privileges of their respective members and the inviolability of the site where they gather to session.

Micronesia (1978-1990)

Section 15

A member of Congress is privileged from arrest during his attendance at Congress and while going to and from sessions, except for treason, felony, or breach of the peace. A member answers only to Congress for his statements in Congress.

The Republic of Moldova (1994-2002)

Article 70

(3) Except in cases of flagrant infringement of law members of Parliament may not be detained for questioning, put under arrest, searched or put on trial without Parliament's assent, after prior hearing of the member in question.

Article 71

Members of Parliament may not be prosecuted or tried by law for their votes of opinions expressed in the exercise of their mandate.

Monaco (1962-2002)

Article 56

The members of the National Council shall not incur any civil or criminal liability by reason of the opinions or the votes they express in the exercise of their mandate. They shall not, without authorization of the Council, be prosecuted nor arrested during a session by reason of a criminal or correctional infraction, except in the case of flagrant offense.

Mongolia (1992-2001)

Article 22

2. Immunity of members of the State Great Hural shall be protected by law.

3. The State Great Hural, meeting in plenary, shall debate questions concerning the involvement of one of its members in a crime to decide on the suspension of his/her mandate. If a court rules that the member is guilty, it shall end his/her term of office.

Montenegro (October 22, 2007)

Article 86

Member of the Parliament shall enjoy immunity.

Member of the Parliament shall not be called to criminal or other account or detained because of the expressed opinion or vote in the perfoamance of his/her duty as a Member of Parliament.

No penal action shall be taken against and no detention shall be assigned to a Member of the Parliament, without the consent of the Parliament, unless the Member has been caught performing a criminal offence for which there is a prescribed sentence of over five years of imprisonment.

The President of Montenegro, the Prime Minister and members of the Government, the President of the Supreme Court, the President and the judges of the Constitutional Court, and the Supreme State Prosecutor shall enjoy the same immunity as the Member of the Parliament.

Morocco (1996)

Article 39

No member of Parliament can be prosecuted or pursued, detained or tried for opinions or votes expressed in the exercise of his functions, except in case the expressed opinions put in question the monarchical system, the Muslim religion or lack respect due to the King.

No member of Parliament can be prosecuted or arrested, during the sessions, for crimes or misdemeanors, other than those indicated in the preceding paragraph without the authorization of the Chamber to which he belongs, except in case of a flagrant crime.

No member of Parliament can be arrested during the recess without the authorization of the Bureau of the Chamber to which he belongs, except in case of flagrant crime, and in authorized prosecutions or definitive condemnation.

The detention or prosecution of a member of Parliament is suspended, if the Chamber to which he belongs requests it, except in case[s] of flagrant crime, authorized prosecutions, or definitive condemnation.

Mozambique (1990)

Article 144

1. No deputy to the People's Assembly may be arrested, unless apprehended in the very act of committing a criminal offence. No deputy may be brought to trial without the consent of the Assembly or of its Standing Commission.

2. Deputies to the People's Assembly shall be tried by the Supreme Court.

Article 145

1. Deputies to the People's Assembly may not be sued, detained, or put on trial for opinions voiced or votes cast in exercising their function as deputies.

2. The above does not apply to civil or criminal responsibility for defamation or slander.

Union of Myanmar (Burma)

As of 1988 the government and country is controlled by the State Law and Restoration Council.

Namibia (1990-1998)

Article 60

3) Rules providing for the privileges and immunities of members of the National Assembly shall be made by Act of Parliament and all members shall be entitled to the protection of such privileges and immunities.

Powers, Privileges and Immunities of Parliament Act. 1996

2. Notwithstanding the provisions of any law, no member shall be liable to any civil or criminal proceedings, arrest, imprisonment, or damages by reason of -

(a) anything done in the exercise of that member's right to freedom of speech in Parliament;

(b) any matter or thing which such member -

(i) brought by report, petition, bill, resolution, motion or otherwise in or before Parliament;

(ii) said in Parliament, whether as a member or a witness, or otherwise may have communicated while taking part in any proceedings in Parliament.

Nauru (1968)

Article 37

The powers, privileges and immunities of Parliament and of its members and committees are such as are declared by Parliament.

No further legislative information is available; however the Comparative Reference Compendium of the Inter-Parliamentary Union of 1986 suggests that the Members follow the Westminster model.

Nepal (1990)

Article 62

(1) Subject to the provisions of this Constitution, there shall be full freedom of speech in both Houses of Parliament and no member shall be arrested, detained or prosecuted in any court for anything said or any vote cast in the House.

(6) No member of Parliament shall be arrested between the date of issuance of the summons for a session and the date on which that session closes:

Provided that nothing in this clause shall be deemed to prevent the arrest under any law of any member on a criminal charge. If any member is so arrested, the official making such arrest shall forthwith inform the person chairing the concerned House.

The Netherlands (1983)

Article 71

(1884)

Members of the States General, Ministers, State Secretaries and other persons taking part in deliberations may not be prosecuted or otherwise held liable in law for anything they say during the sittings of the States General or of its committees or for anything they submit to them in writing.

New Zealand (1908)

Article 242

Privileges of House of Representatives

(1) [The House of Representatives]... and the Committees and members thereof... shall hold, enjoy, and exercise such and the like privileges, immunities, and powers as on the 1st day of January 1865 were held, enjoyed, and exercised by the Commons House of Parliament of Great Britain and Ireland, and by the Committees and members thereof, so far as the same are not inconsistent with or repugnant to such of the provisions of the Constitutions Act as on the 26th day of September 1865 (being the date of the coming into operation of the Parliamentary Privileges Act 1865) were unrepealed, whether such privileges, immunities, or powers were so held, possessed, or enjoyed by custom, statute, or otherwise.

Nicaragua (1986-1995)

Article 139

Deputies shall be exempt from responsibility for their opinions and votes cast in the National Assembly and enjoy immunity in conformity with the law.

Unofficial Translation
Law (no 83) of Immunity of March 21, 1990

1.(b) While exercising their duties, the following enjoy immunity:
- propriety representatives and witnesses before the National Assembly

These functionaries cannot be the object of judicial or prejudicial action before the tribunals of the public while exercising their duty.

4. Ex representatives before the National Assembly elected since the election of 1984 will enjoy immunity during the year after they cease their functions.

5. Those persons who consider that they have been affected by persons mentioned in Article 4, whether the nature of the injury is personal or public, have recourse to the National Assembly in the case of ex representatives and witnesses.

7. Those functionaries (propriety representatives, witnesses and ex representatives) who enjoy immunity may renounce this privilege when the case is presented if they consider it to be the correct thing to do.

8. When the secretary of the National Assembly receives the complaint which has been presented he/she shall inform the executive powers of the National Assembly for processing.

13. If the National Assembly accepts the complaint with a minimum of 60% of the votes of Members, it will proceed. If the complaint is rejected, there is no possibility of reintroducing the same complaint.

15. The functionary who enjoys immunity may be detained if he has been found in *flagrante delicto* and will remain in prison until the National Assembly decides on the matter within 60 days.

Niger (1999)

Article 70

The members of the National Assembly enjoy parliamentary immunity.

No deputy may be prosecuted, searched, arrested, detained or judged on the basis of the opinions or the votes expressed by him in the exercise of his functions.

Except in case of flagrant offence, no deputy can be prosecuted or arrested, during the period of the sessions, in matters of misdemeanors or serious crimes except with the authorization of the National Assembly.

A deputy may be arrested out of session only with the authorization of the Bureau of the National Assembly, except in case of flagrant offence, of authorized prosecutions or of final condemnations.

Nigeria (1999)

Legislative Houses (Power and Privileges Act) Cap 208 of the Laws of the Federation 1990 and 1991
Section 3

No civil or criminal proceedings may be instituted against any member of a legislative House.

a. In respect of words spoken before that house or a Committee thereof; or

b. in respect of words written in a report to that House, to any Committee thereof or in any petition, bill, resolution, motion or question brought or introduced by him therein.

Norway (1814)

Article 66

Representatives on their way to and from the Storting, as well as during their attendance there, shall be exempt from personal arrest, unless they are apprehended in public crimes, nor may they be called to account outside the meetings of the Storting for opinions expressed there. Every representative shall be bound to conform to the rules of procedure therein adopted.

Oman (1996)

Sultani Decree No. (101-96)
Promulgating the Basic Statute of the State
(Based on Islamic Sharia)

Pakistan (1973-1990)

Article 66

(1) Subject to the Constitution and to the rules of procedure of Majlis-e-Shoora (Parliament), there shall be freedom of speech in Majlis-e-Shoora (Parliament) and no member shall be liable to any proceedings in any court in respect of anything said or any vote given by him in Majlis-e-Shoora

(Parliament), and no person shall be so liable in respect of the publication by or under the authority of Majlis-e-Shoora (Parliament) of any report, paper, votes or proceedings.

(2) In other respects, the powers, immunities and privileges of Majlis-e-Shoora (Parliament), and the immunities and privileges of the members of Majlis-e-Shoora (Parliament), shall be such as may from time to time be defined by law and, until so defined, shall be such as were, immediately before the commencing day, enjoyed by the National Assembly of Pakistan and the committees thereof and its members.

Palau (1981-1992)

Section 9

No member of either house of the Olbiil Era Kelulau shall be held to answer in any other place for any speech or debate in the Olbiil Era Kelulau. The members of the Olbiil Era Kelulau shall be privileged, in all cases except treason, felony, or breach of peace, from arrest during their attendance at the sessions of the Olbiil Era Kelulau and in going to and from the sessions.

Panama (1972-1994)

Article 148

Members of the Legislative Assembly are not legally responsible for opinions expressed or votes given in the discharge of their duties.

Article 149

Five days before the period of each Legislature, during it, and up to five days after, members of the Legislative Assembly shall be granted immunity. In such a period they may not be prosecuted or arrested for penal or police reasons without prior authorization by the Legislative Assembly.

Papua New Guinea (1975-1995)

Article 115

(1) The powers (other than legislative powers), privileges and immunities of the Parliament and of its members and committees are as prescribed by or under this section and by any other provision of this Constitution.

(2) There shall be freedom of speech, debate and proceeding in the Parliament, and the exercise of those freedoms shall not be questioned in any court or in any proceedings whatever (otherwise than in proceedings in the Parliament or before a committee of the Parliament).

(3) No member of the Parliament is subject to the jurisdiction of any court in respect of the exercise of his powers or the performance of his functions, duties or responsibilities as such, but this subsection does not affect the operation of Division III.2 (*leadership code*).

(4) No member of the Parliament is liable to civil or criminal proceedings, arrest, imprisonment, fine, damages or compensation by reason of any matter or thing that he has brought by petition, question, bill, resolution, motion or otherwise, or has said before or submitted to the Parliament or a committee of the Parliament.

(5) No member of the Parliament or other person is liable to civil or criminal proceedings, arrest, imprisonment, fine, damages or compensation by reason of –

(a) an act done under the authority of the Parliament or under an order of the Parliament or a committee of the Parliament; or

(b) words spoken or used, or a document or writing made or produced, under an order or summons made or issued under the authority of the Parliament or a committee of the Parliament.

(6) Members of the Parliament are free from arrest for civil debt during meetings of the Parliament and during the period commencing three days before, and ending

three days after, a meeting when they are travelling from their respective electorates to attend the meeting or are returning to their electorates from the meeting.

Paraguay (1992)

Article 191

No charges may be pressed in court against a member of Congress for the opinions he may have expressed in discharging his duties. No senator or deputy may be arrested from the day of his election until the end of his term, unless he is caught in flagrante delicto in relation to a crime meriting a prison sentence. In this case, the official intervening in the case will place the legislator under house arrest and will immediately report the arrest to the respective chamber and to a competent judge, to whom he will submit the case files as soon as possible.

If a court of law orders a pretrial inquest against a senator or a deputy, the presiding judge will send a copy of the case tiles to the respective chamber, which will examine the merits of the inquest and, by a two-thirds majority vote, will decide whether the senator or deputy involved should be stripped of his immunity in order to stand trial. If the chamber votes against the legislator, it will suspend his immunity so that he may be brought to trial.

Peru

Article 93

They are not responsible before any authority or court for opinions held and votes cast in the exercise of their functions.

They may not be prosecuted or arrested without prior authorization of the Congress or its Standing Committee [Comisión Permanente]. Congressmen have tenure from the time of their election to a month after terminating their functions, except for an offense caught in the act, in which case they are placed at the disposal of the Congress or its

Standing Committee within 24 hours to determine whether their imprisonment and trial may be authorized or not.

Republic of the Philippines (1986)

Section 11

A Senator or Member of the House of Representatives shall, in all offenses punishable by not more than six years imprisonment, be privileged from arrest while the Congress is in session. No Member shall be questioned nor be held liable in any other place for any speech or debate in the Congress or in any committee thereof.

Poland (1992)

Article 105

1. A Deputy cannot be held accountable for his activity performed within the scope of a Deputy's mandate during the tern or after its completion. Regarding such activities, a Deputy can only be held accountable before the Sejm and, in a case where he had infringed the rights of third parties, he may only be proceeded against before a court with the consent of the Sejm.

2. From the day of announcement of the results of the elections until the day of the expiry of his mandate, a Deputy cannot be subjected to criminal accountability without the consent of the Sejm.

3. Criminal proceedings instituted against a person before the day of his election as Deputy shall be suspended at the request of the Sejm until the time of expiry of the mandate. In such case, the statute of limitation with respect to criminal proceedings shall be extended for a corresponding time.

4. A Deputy can consent to be brought to criminal accountability. In such case, the provisions of paragraphs 2 and 3 shall not apply.

5. A Deputy cannot be detained or arrested without the consent of the Sejm, except for cases in flagrante

delicto and in which this detention is necessary for securing the proper course of proceedings. Any such detention shall be immediately communicated to the Marshal of the Sejm, who may order an immediate release of the Deputy.

6. Detailed principles and procedures for bringing Deputies to criminal accountability are provided by law.

Portugal (1976)

Article 157

1. Deputies are not subject to civil, criminal or disciplinary proceedings with respect to their voting or opinions expressed in the performance of their duties.

2. Deputies may not be heard as witnesses or as defendants without the permission of the Assembly. In the latter case permission shall be obligatory when there is strong evidence that a serious crime has been committed that is punishable with a maximum sentence of imprisonment for more than three years.

3. No Deputies can be detained or arrested unless on the authority of the Assembly or when found in *flagrante delicto* committing a crime punishable by imprisonment as set out in the above paragraph.

4. When criminal proceedings are institutes against a Deputy who is charged with an offense, the Assembly shall decide whether or not the Deputy shall be suspended so that the proceedings can proceed. The decision to suspend shall be obligatory when it concerns a crime refereed to in the above paragraph.

Amirate of Qatar (1973)

The Constitution provides for a Ruler,
a Council of Ministers and an Advisory Council.

Romania (1991)

Article 69

1. A deputy or senator cannot be detained, arrested, searched, or charged with a penal offense or contravention without the consent of the chamber to which he belongs, after giving him a hearing. The competence for the judgement rests with the Supreme Court of Justice.

2. In the case of a capital crime, the deputy or the senator can be detained and searched. The Ministry of Justice will immediately inform the president of the chamber about the detention and search. If the chamber notified finds that there are not grounds for the detention, it will order the immediate revocation of this measure.

Article 70

Deputies and senators cannot be held legally responsible for their votes or for the political views expressed in the exercise of their mandate.

Russian Federation (1993)

Article 98

1. Deputies for the Federation Council and deputies to the State Duma possess immunity throughout their term in office. They cannot be detained, arrested, searched except when detained in the act of perpetrating a crime, and may not be subject to personal search except when such search is authorized by law to ensure the safety of other people.

2. The question of depriving a deputy of immunity shall be decided on the recommendation of the Prosecutor-General of the Russian Federation by the corresponding chamber of the Federal Assembly.

Rwanda (1991)

Article 66

Deputies may not be prosecuted or accused because of opinions or votes expressed by them in the exercise of their duties.

Except in case of flagrante delicto, Deputies may be prosecuted or arrested for other acts, or be subject to civil imprisonment only by authorization from the National Assembly passed by secret ballot by a majority of ¾ of its members.

Prosecution or imprisonment resulting from flagrante delicto or from authorization from the National Assembly shall be suspended during the session period if required by the National Assembly by a majority of ¾ of its members and by secret ballot, except in case of a definite conviction. Deputies shall be subject to the Court of Cassation which shall rule, all chambers assembled, as the first and final resort.

St. Christopher and Nevis (1983)

Article 45

Without prejudice to any provision made by Parliament relating to the powers, privileges and immunities of the National Assembly and its committees, or the privileges and immunities of the members and officers of the Assembly and of other persons concerned in the business of the Assembly or its committees, no civil or criminal proceedings may be instituted against any member of the Assembly or a committee thereof or by reason of any matter or thing brought by him therein by petition, bill, resolution, motion or otherwise.

St. Lucia (1978)

Article 42

Without prejudice to any provision made by Parliament relating to the powers, privileges and immunities of the Senate or the House and the committees thereof, or the privileges and immunities of the members and officers of the Senate or the House and of other persons concerned in the business of the Senate or the House or the committees thereof, no civil or criminal proceedings may be instituted against any member of the Senate or the House for words spoken before, or written in a report to, the Senate or the House or a committee thereof or by reason of any matter or thing brought by him therein by petition, bill, resolution, motion or otherwise.

St. Vincent (1979)

Article 46

Without prejudice to any provision made by Parliament relating to the powers, privileges, and immunities of the House and its committees, or the privileges and immunities of the members and officers of the House and of other persons concerned in the business of the House or its committees, no civil or criminal proceedings may be instituted against any member of the House for words spoken before, or written in a report to, the House or a committee thereof or by reason of any matter or thing brought by him therein by petition, bill, resolution, motion or otherwise.

Samoa (1960-2000)

Article 62

The privileges, immunities and powers of the Legislative Assembly, of the committees thereof and of Members of Parliament may be determined by Act: Provided that no such privilege or power may extend to the imposition of a fine or to committal to prison for contempt or otherwise, unless provision is made by Act for the trial and punishment of the person concerned by the Supreme Court.

The Legislative Assembly Powers and Privileges Ordinance, 1960

3. Immunity from proceedings – No member of the Legislative Assembly shall be laible to any civil or criminal proceedings in respect of:

(a) Any speech or debate in the Legislative Assembly or a committee thereof;

(b) Any words written in a report to the Assembly or any committee thereof or in any petition, bill, motion or other matter brought or introduced by him therein.

4. Immunity from imprisonment or restraint – No member of the Legislative Assembly, unless by order or sentence of the Legislative Assembly, shall be liable to imprisonment during his attendance at the Legislative Assembly or a committee thereof and during a period not exceeding 2 days while going to and the like period while returning from any meeting of the Legislative Assembly or a committee thereof in consequence of conviction of any criminal offence, not being an offence punishable by death or imprisonment for 2 years or more, and not being a refusal to enter into a recognisance for keeping peace.

Sâo Tomé and Principe (1975-1990)

Article 84

1. No Deputy may be inconvenienced, pursued, detained, imprisoned, judged or condemned for votes and opinions he may make during the exercise of his duties.

2. Except in the instance of flagrante delicto and for a crime punishable as a felony and by consent of the National Assembly or of its Permanent Commission, Deputies may not be pursued or imprisoned for crimes committed outside their duties.

Saudi Arabia

The Sharia rules and provides basic Islamic system.

Senegal (1962-1999)

Article 50

No member of Parliament may be prosecuted, sought, arrested, detained or judged as a result of the opinions [expressed] or votes cast by him in the exercise of his functions.

No member of Parliament may, during the sessions, be prosecuted or arrested in a criminal or correctional matter, without the authorization of the Assembly or which he is a part except in the case of flagrant offense. No member of Parliament may, out of session, be arrested without the authorization of the Bureau of the Assembly of which he is a part, except in the case of flagrant offense, authorized prosecutions, or a definitive conviction.

The detention or the prosecution of a member of Parliament is suspended if the Assembly of which he is a part requires it.

Serbia/Montenegro (1990)

Article 24

Members of Parliament shall enjoy freedom of speech in the Parliament of Serbia and Montenegro and immunity for words spoken and acts done in the performance of their duties as Member of Parliament.

A Member of Parliament may not be made accountable, arrested or punished without the approval of the Parliament of Serbia and Montenegro, unless he/she has been caught in the act of committing a crime punishable by an imprisonment of five or more years.

The President of Serbia and Montenegro, members of the Council of Ministers and the judges of the Court of Serbia and Montenegro enjoy the same immunities as members of Parliament.

Republic of Seychelles (1993)

Article 102

(1) There shall be freedom of speech and debate in the National Assembly and a member shall not be subject to the jurisdiction of any court or to any proceedings whatsoever, other than in proceedings in the Assembly, when exercising those freedoms or performing the functions of a member in the Assembly.

(2) Where the National Assembly is in session an arrest shall not be effected against a member in a way which will interfere with the performance by the member of the functions of the member in the Assembly and, where proceedings are instituted against a member, the court or authority before which the proceedings are being conducted shall so conduct the proceedings as to allow the member to continue to perform the functions of the member in the Assembly.

(3) Where an arrest has been effected against a member, or any proceedings against a member begun, before the beginning of the session of the Assembly, the arrest or proceedings shall not be allowed to interfere with the performance by the member of the functions of the member in the Assembly.

(4) The protection afforded under clauses (2) and (3) shall, in the case of a criminal proceedings, end upon the court or authority before which the proceedings are being conducted passing a sentence on the member on the conviction of the member.

Sierra Leone (1991)

Article 98

There shall be freedom of speech, debate and proceedings in Parliament and that freedom shall not be impeached or questioned in any court or place out of Parliament.

Article 99

(1) Subject to the provisions of this section, but without prejudice to the generality of section 97, no civil or criminal proceedings shall be instituted against a Member of Parliament in any court or place out of Parliament by reason of anything said by him in Parliament.

(2) Whenever in the opinion of the person presiding in Parliament a statement made by a Member is *prima facie* defamatory of any person, the person presiding shall refer the matter for inquiry to the Committee of Privileges which shall report its findings to Parliament not later than thirty days of the matter being so referred.

Singapore (1963-2001)

Constitution
Article 63

It shall be lawful for the Legislature by law to determine and regulate the privileges, immunities or powers of Parliament.

Parliament (Privileges, Immunities and Powers) Act

3. (1) The privileges, immunities and powers of Parliament and of the Speaker, Members and committees of Parliament shall be the same as those of the Commons House of Parliament of the United Kingdom and of its Speaker, Members or committees as the establishment of the Republic of Singapore.

5. There shall be freedom of speech and debate and proceedings in Parliament, and such freedom of speech and debate and proceedings shall not be liable to be impeached or questioned in any court, commission inquiry, tribunal or any other place whatsoever out of Parliament.

6. (1) No Member shall be liable to any civil or criminal proceedings, arrest, imprisonment or damages by reason of any matter or thing which he may have brought before Parliament or a committee by petition, bill, resolution, motion, or otherwise or may have said in Parliament or in committee.

Slovakia (1992)

Article 78

(1) No deputy shall be prosecuted for his vote in the National Council or its committees, and this even after the expiration of his mandate.

(2) For statements made in the National Council of the Slovak Republic in the exercise of the function of deputy, no deputy can be criminally prosecuted and this even after the expiration of his mandate. The deputy is subject to the disciplinary powers of the National Council of the Slovak Republic. The responsibility of the deputy under civil law is not affected thereby.

(3) A deputy cannot be criminally or disciplinarily prosecuted, not taken into custody without the approval of the National Council of the Slovak Republic. If the National Council rejects a criminal prosecution or an arrest is excluded for the duration of the mandate of the deputy, in such a case the suspension of his mandate does not count.

(4) If a deputy was apprehended and detained while committing a criminal offence, the competent organ is obligated to inform immediately the Chairman of the National Council of the Slovak Republic. If the mandate and community committee does not give the required approval for the arrest, the deputy must be immediately released.

(5) If the deputy is in custody his mandate does not end, but is not taken into account.

Slovenia (1991)

Article 83

A deputy of the State Assembly is not criminally liable for any opinions expressed or any vote cast at sessions of the State Assembly or its working bodies.

A deputy may not be detained nor may criminal proceedings be initiated against him, where such deputy claims immunity, without the permission of the State Assembly, except if he has been apprehended committing a criminal offence for which a prison sentence of over five years is prescribed. The State Assembly may also grant immunity to a deputy who has not claimed it or who has been apprehended committing such criminal offence referred to in the preceding paragraph.

Solomon Islands (1978)

Article 62

Subject to the provisions of this Constitution, Parliament may from time to time make, amend and revoke rules and orders for the regulation and orderly conduct of its proceedings and the dispatch of business, and for the passing, intituling and numbering of Bills.

Article 69

Parliament may prescribe the privileges, immunities and powers of Parliament and its members.

Standing Orders of the Solomon Islands

25. Matters of Privilege

(1) A Member who wishes to raise a matter which he believes affects the privileges of Parliament may, not later than the day before the sitting at which he wishes to raise the matter, inform the Speaker of his wish, stating the facts to which he wishes to draw attention.

Somalia

There is neither an elected government
nor a constitution in Somalia at present.

South Africa (1996)

Article 58

(1) Cabinet members [Deputy Ministers] and members of the National Assembly –

(a) have freedom of speech in the Assembly and in its committees, subject to is rules and orders; and

(b) are not liable to civil or criminal proceedings, arrest, imprisonment or damages for-

(i) anything that they have said in, produced before or submitted to the Assembly or any of its committees; or

(ii) anything revealed as a result of anything that they have said in, produced before or submitted to the Assembly or any of its committees.

(2) Other privileges and immunities of the National Assembly, Cabinet members and members of the Assembly may be prescribed by national legislation.

Spain (1978)

Article 71

1. The Deputies and Senators enjoy inviolability for the opinions expressed during the exercise of their functions.

2. During the period of their mandate, the Deputies and Senators enjoy immunity and may only be arrested in case of 'flagrante delicto.' They may not be indicted or tried without prior authorization of the respective Chamber.

3. In actions against Deputies and Senators, the Criminal Section of the Supreme Court shall be competent.

Sri Lanka (1972-1988)

Article 67

The privileges, immunities, and powers of Parliament and of its Members may be determined and regulated by

Parliament by law, and until so determined and regulated, the provisions of the Parliament (Powers and Privileges) Act, shall, *mutates mutandis*, apply.

Parliament (Powers and Privileges) Act, Part I

3. There shall be freedom of speech, debate and proceeding in Parliament and such freedom of speech, debate or proceedings shall not be liable to be impeached or questioned in any court or place out of Parliament.

4. No member shall be liable to any civil or criminal proceedings, arrest, imprisonment, or damages by reason of anything which he may have said in Parliament or by reason of any matter or thing which he may have brought before Parliament by petition, bill, resolution, motion or otherwise.

5. Except for a contravention of this Act, no member shall be liable to arrest, detention, or molestation in respect of any debt or matter which may be the subject of civil proceeding while proceeding to, or in attendance at, or returning from, any meeting or sitting of Parliament: Provided that any person otherwise entitled to any immunity or privilege under this section who shall be deemed to have committed any act of insolvency may be dealt with under the Insolvency Ordinance as if he had not such immunity or privilege.

7. Parliament and the members thereof shall hold, enjoy and exercise, in addition to the privileges, immunities and powers conferred by this Act, such and the like immunities as are for the time being held, enjoyed and exercised by the Commons House of the Parliament of the United Kingdom and by the members thereof.

Sudan (1977-1998)

Article 74

Save where he is in the very act of crime, no criminal proceedings shall be initiated against a member of the National Assembly, not shall any of the detection measures be taken against his person, residence or belongings without permission from the Speaker of the Assembly.

Suriname (1987)

Article 88

The chairman, the members of the National Assembly, the Government and the experts referred to in article 85, paragraph (2), shall be exempt from criminal prosecution for anything they have said at the assembly or have submitted to it in writing, except that if in so doing they had made public what was said or submitted under obligation of secrecy in a closed meeting.

Swaziland (1968)

Section 62

(1) Subject to the provisions of this Constitution, the King and Parliament may make laws for the peace, order and good government of Swaziland.

(2) Subsection (1) of this section shall not apply to the matters specified in Schedule 3 to this Constitution, which shall continue to be regulated by Swazi law and custom: Provided that, with the consent of the Swazi National Council signified in writing under the hand of the Secretary of that Council, the King and Parliament may make laws with respect to any such matter that is specified in the writing.

No further information is available.

Sweden (1974)

Article 8

No person may institute criminal proceedings against a person who holds a mandate as a member of the Riksdag, or who has held such a mandate, deprive him of liberty, or take action to restrict his movements within the Realm on account of an act or statement made in the exercise of his mandate, unless the Riksdag has given its consent thereto in a decision in which at least five sixths of those voting concur. If in any other case a member of the Riksdag is suspected of having committed a criminal act, the relevant rules of law concerning arrest, detention or remand shall be applied only if he admits guilt or was caught in the act, or the minimum penalty for the offence is imprisonment for at least two years.

Switzerland

Article 162

1. The members of the Federal Assembly and the Federal Council, as well as the Federal Chancellor may not be held responsible for their statements in the Chambers and before parliamentary organs.

2. The law may provide for further forms of immunity, and extend them to other persons.

Loi du 13 décembre 2002 sur l'Assemblée fédérale (Loi sur le Parlement, LParl)

Article 16

Aucun député ne peut être tenu pour juridiquement responsable des propos qu'il tient devant les conseils ou leurs organes.

Article 17

1. Un député soupçonné d'avoir commis une infraction en rapport avec ses fonctions ou ses activités parlementaires ne peut être poursuivi qu'avec l'autorisation de l'Assemblée fédérale.

2. La demande de lever l'immunité d'un député est examinée d'abord par le conseil dont il est membre.

3. Le député en cause est entendu par les commissions chargées de l'examen préalable.

4. Si des circonstances particulières le justifient, l'Assemblée fédérale peut renvoyer le député en cause devant le Tribunal fédéral, même si l'infraction présumée relève de la juridiction cantonale. En pareil

cas, l'Assemblée fédérale (Chambres réunies) désigne un procureur général extraordinaire.

Syria (1973-2000)

Article 66

Members of the Assembly are not accountable before criminal or civil courts for any occurrences or views they express, in voting in public or secret sessions, or in the activities of the various committees.

Article 67

Members of the Assembly enjoy immunity throughout the term of the Assembly. Unless they are apprehended in the act of committing a crime, no penal measures can be taken against any member without the advance permission of the Assembly. When the Assembly is not in session, permission must be obtained from the President of the Assembly. As soon as it convenes, the Assembly shall be notified of the measures taken.

Taiwan (1947-2000)

Article 73

No Member of the Legislative Yuan shall be held responsible outside the Yuan for opinions expressed or votes cast in the Yuan.

Article 74

No Member of the Legislative Yuan shall, except in case of flagrante delicto, be arrested or detained without the permission of the Legislative Yuan.

Tajikistan (2003)

Article 51

A member of the Majlisi Milli and a deputy of the Majlisi Namoyandagon are independent of the will of the electorate [and] have the right to freely express their opinion and to vote according to their conviction.

A member of the Majlisi Milly and a deputy of the Majlisi Namoyandagon have the right to immunity; he may not be arrested, detained, taken into custody, [and] searched, except in cases of detainment at a scene of a crime. A member of the Majlisi Milly and a deputy of the Majlisi Namoyandagon may not be subjected to a personal search except in cases provided for by law in order to ensure safety of other people. Issues regarding the deprivation of a member of the Majlisi Milly and a deputy of the Majlisi Namoyandagon of their immunity are resolved by the corresponding Majlisi upon a presentation of the General Procurator.

Tanzania (1998)

Article 100

(1) There shall be freedom of opinion, debate and in the National Assembly, and that freedom shall not be breached or questioned by any organ in the United Republic or in any court or elsewhere outside the National Assembly.

(2) Subject to this Constitution or to the provisions of any other relevant law, a Member of Parliament shall not be prosecuted and no civil proceedings may be instituted against him in a court in relation to any thing which he has said or done in the National Assembly or has submitted to the National Assembly by way of petition, bill, motion or otherwise.

Article 101

Parliament may enact a law making provisions to enable the court and the law to preserve and enforce freedom of opinion, debate and procedure of business in the National Assembly which in terms of Article 100 is guaranteed by this Constitution.

Thailand (1991-1995)

Section 157

At a sitting of the House of Representatives or the Senate or at a joint sitting of the National Assembly, words expressed in giving statements of fact or opinions or in casting the vote by any member are absolutely privileged. No charge or action in any manner whatsoever shall be brought against such member.

The privilege under Paragraph One does not extend to a member who expressed words at a sitting which is broadcast through radio or television if such words appear outside the premises of the National Assembly and the expression of such words constitutes a criminal offense of a wrongful act against any other person, who is not a Minister or member of that House.

In the case of Paragraph Two, if the words expressed by the member cause damage to another person who is not a Minister or member of that House, the President of that House shall cause explanations to be published as requested by that person in accordance with procedure and within such period of time as prescribed in the rules of the procedure of the House, without prejudice to the person's right to bring the case before the Court.

Togo (1960-2002)

Article 53

The Deputies of the National Assembly shall enjoy parliamentary immunity.

No Deputy shall be prosecuted, searched, detained, confined or passed judgment upon because of his opinions or voting record in the exercise of his duties, even after he has completed his term of office.

Except in the case of a flagrant offense, Deputies shall not be able to be detained or prosecuted for crimes and other misdemeanors except when their parliamentary immunity is lifted by the National Assembly.

Any proceedings relating to a flagrant offense which are brought against a Deputy shall be reported immediately to the Office of the National Assembly.

When the National Assembly is not in session, no Deputy shall be able to be detained without authorization from the Assembly's Office.

Any confinement or prosecution of a Deputy shall be suspended at the request of the National Assembly.

Tonga (1875-1991)

Article 73

The members of the Legislative Assembly shall be free from arrest and judgment whilst it is sitting except for indictable offences and no member of the House shall be liable for anything his may have said or published in the Legislative Assembly.

Trinidad and Tobago (1962-1988)

Section 55

(1) Subject to the provisions of this Constitution and to the rules and standing orders regulating to the procedure of the Senate and House of Representatives, there shall be freedom of speech in the Senate and House of Representatives.

(2) No civil or criminal proceedings may be instituted against any member of either House for words spoken before, or written in a report to, the House of which he is a member or in which he has a right of audience under section 62 or a committee thereof or any joint committee or meeting of the Senate and House of Representatives or by reason of any matter or thing brought by him therein by petition, bill, resolution, motion or otherwise; or for the publication by or under the authority of either House of any report, paper, votes or proceedings.

(3) In other respects, the powers, privileges and immunities of each House and of the members and the committees of each House, shall be such as may from time to time be prescribed by Parliament after the commencement of the this Constitution and until so defined shall be those of the House of Commons of the Parliament of the United Kingdom and of its members and committees at the commencement of this Constitution.

(4) A person called to give any evidence before either House or any committee shall enjoy the same privileges and immunities as a member of either House.

Tunisia (1959-1988)

Article 26

The deputy cannot be prosecuted, arrested or tried for opinions expressed, proposals made or acts carried out in the exercise of his mandate in the Chamber of Deputies.

Article 27

No deputy can be arrested or prosecuted for the duration of his mandate for a crime or misdemeanor as long as the Chamber of Deputies has not lifter the immunity which covers him. However, in the even of flagrant crime, arrest procedure is permitted, in such a case, the Chamber of Deputies is (to be) informed without delay. The detention of a deputy is suspended if the Deputies so requests.

Turkey (1982-2002)

Article 83

Members of the Grand National Assembly of Turkey cannot be liable for their votes and statements concerning parliamentary functions, for the views they express before the Assembly, or unless the Assembly decides otherwise on the proposal of the Bureau for that sitting, for repeating or revealing these outside the Assembly.

A deputy, who is alleged to have committed an offence before or after election, cannot be arrested, interrogated, detained or tried unless the Assembly decides otherwise. This provision does not apply in cases where a member is caught in the act of committing an offence punishable by a heavy penalty and in cases subject to Article 14 of the Constitution if an investigation has been initiated before the election. However, in such situations the competent authority notifies the Grand National Assembly of Turkey immediately and directly.

The execution of a criminal sentence imposed on a member of the Grand National Assembly of Turkey either before or after his election is suspended until he ceases to be a member; the statute of limitations does not apply during the term of membership.

Investigation and prosecution of a re-elected deputy can be subject to whether or not the Assembly lifts immunity in the cast of the individual involved.

Political party groups in the Grand National Assembly of Turkey not hold discussions or take decisions regarding parliamentary immunity.

Turkmenistan (1992-1999)

Article 70

A deputy may be deprived of his deputy powers only by the Mejlis. Any decision on that issue is adopted by a majority of no less than two thirds of the deputies of the Mejlis. A deputy may not be subjected to criminal prosecution, arrested or in another manner deprived of freedom without the consent of the Mejlis or the Presidium of the Mejlis during the period between sessions.

Tuvalu (1986)

Section 114

(1) The purpose of this section is to allow, as is customary in Parliaments –

(a) certain privileges and immunities to be conferred upon Parliament and members of Parliament; and

(b) certain powers to be conferred upon Parliament, in order to facilitate the proper conduct of the business of Parliament, and to prevent improper interference with the conduct of that business.

(2) Subject to subsections (4) and (5), Parliament may provide for –

(a) privileges and immunities of Parliament and members of Parliament; and

(b) powers of Parliament.

(3) Any provision made by Parliament made for the purposes of subsection (2) shall be interpreted and applied only in accordance with the purpose of this section as set out in subsection (1).

(4) No civil or criminal proceedings may be instituted against a member of Parliament –

(a) for words spoken in, or included in a report to, Parliament of a committee of Parliament; or

(b) by reason of any matter or thing brought by him in Parliament or a committee of Parliament.

(5) No process issued by a court shall be served or issued within the precincts of Parliament (as defined by or under an Act of Parliament or the Rules of Procedure of Parliament).

Uganda (1967-1995)

Article 97

The Speaker, the Deputy Speaker, members of Parliament and any other person participating or assisting in or acting in connection with or reporting the proceedings of Parliament or any of its committees shall be entitled to such immunities and privileges as Parliament shall by law prescribe.

No further information is available.

Ukraine (1996)

Article 80

National Deputies of Ukraine are guaranteed parliamentary immunity.

National Deputies of Ukraine are not legally liable for the results of voting or for statements made in Parliament and in its bodies, with the exception of liability for insult of defamation. National Deputies of Ukraine shall not be held criminally liable, detained or arrested without the consent of the Verkhovna Rada of Ukraine.

United Arab Emirates (1971)

Article 81

Members of the Council shall not be censured for any opinions or views expressed in the course of carrying out their duties within the Council or its Committees.

Article 82

No penal proceedings may be instituted against any member while the Council is in session, except in cases of 'flagrante delicto', without the permission of the Council. The Council must be informed if such proceedings are instituted while it is not in session.

United Kingdom

The Bill of Rights, 1689

Article 9

That the freedom of speech and debates or proceedings in Parliament ought not to be impeached or questioned in any court or place out of Parliament [.]

Section 13 of the Defamation Act, 1996

(1) Where the conduct of a person in or in relation to proceedings in Parliament is in issue in defamation proceedings, he may waive for the purposes of those proceedings, so far as concerns him, the protection

or any enactment of Rule of law which prevents proceedings in Parliament being impeached or questioned in any court or place out of Parliament.

(2) Where a person waives that protection –

(a) any such enactment or rules of law shall not apply to prevent evidence being given, questions being asked or statements, submissions, comments or findings being made about his conduct, and

(b) none of those things shall be regarded as infringing the privilege of either House of Parliament.

(3) The waiver by one person of that protection does not affect its operation in relation to another person who has not waived it.

(4) Nothing in this section affects any enactment or rules of law so far as it protects a person (including a person who has waived the protection referred to above) from legal liability for words spoken or things done in the course of, or for the purposes of or incidental to, any proceedings in Parliament.

United States of America (1787)

Article 1, Section 6

The Senators and Representatives [...] shall in all Cases, except Treason, Felony and Breach of the Peace, be privileged from Arrest during their Attendance at the Session of their respective Houses, and in going to and returning from the same; and for any Speech or Debate in either House, they shall not be questioned in any other Place.

Uruguay (1966-1996)

Article 112

Senators and Representatives shall never be held liable for the votes they cast or opinions expressed during the discharge of their duties.

Article 113

No Senator or Representative, from the day of his election until that of his termination, may be arrested except in case of *flagrante delicto* and then notice shall immediately be given to the respective Chamber, with a summary report of the case.

Article 114

No Senator or Representative, from the day of his election until that of his termination, may be indicted on a criminal charge, or even for common offenses which are not specified in Article 93, except before his own Chamber, which, by tow-thirds of the votes of its full membership, shall decide whether or not there are grounds for prosecution and if so, shall declare him suspended from office and he shall be placed at the disposition of a competent Tribunal.

Uzbekistan (1992)

Article 88

Deputies of the Oliy Majlis shall have the right of immunity. They may not be prosecuted, arrested or incur a court-imposed administrative penalty without the sanction of the Oliy Majlis.

Vanuatu (1980-1983)

Article 27

(1) No member of Parliament may be arrested, detained, prosecuted or proceeded against in respect of opinions given or votes cast by him in Parliament in the exercise of his office.

(2) No member may, during a session of Parliament or of one of its committees, be arrested or prosecuted for any offence, except with the authorization of Parliament in exceptional circumstances.

Venezuela (1999)

Article 199

The deputies to the National Assembly are not responsible for votes and opinions expressed in the performance of their functions. They will only be responsible [*responderán*] before the electors and the legislative body in accordance with the Constitution and the Regulations.

Article 200

The deputies to the National Assembly will enjoy immunity in the performance of their functions from the proclamation until the conclusion of their mandate or the renunciation of the same. The Supreme Tribunal of Justice will hear the alleged crimes that the members of the National Assembly commit, [which is the] only authority that will be able to order, with prior authorization from the National Assembly, their detention and continue their judgment. In case of flagrant crime committed by a parliamentarian, the competent authority will put in him custody in his residence and will communicate the fact to the Supreme Tribunal of Justice.

Vietnam (1989-1992)

Article 99

National Assembly deputies may not be arrested nor prosecuted without the consent of the National Assembly and, when the National Assembly is not in session, without the consent of the National Assembly's Standing Committee. If a National Assembly deputy is temporarily held in custody for a flagrant offense, the interim detaining agency shall immediately report the matter to the National Assembly or its Standing Committee for consideration and decision.

Yemen (1991-1993)

Article 80

No member of the House of Representatives, unless words of scurrility and slander shall be uttered, shall be held liable in respect of anything he said, any vote given by him in public and closed sittings or anything brought up by him to the attention of the House or its committee thereof.

Article 81

No member of the House of Representatives shall be questioned without the prior permission of the House of Representatives excepting cases of flagrante delicto in which case the House of Representatives shall be immediately notified and the House shall ascertain the conformity of the procedures, and in such case as when the House of Representatives shall be in recess, a permission shall be obtained from the Chairmanship Commission of the House of Representatives and, in the next session, the House of Representatives shall be informed in detail of the aforesaid procedures.

Zambia (1991-1996)

Article 87

(1) The National Assembly and its members shall have such privileges, powers and immunities as may be prescribed by an Act of Parliament.

(2) Notwithstanding subclause (1) the law and custom of the Parliament of England shall apply to the National Assembly with such modifications as may be prescribed by or under an Act of Parliament.

Zimbabwe (1974-2000)

Article 49

Subject to the provisions of this Constitution, an Act of Parliament may make provision to determine and regulate the privileges, immunities and powers of Parliament and the members and officers thereof including the Speaker, and to provide penalties for a person who sits or votes in Parliament knowing or having reasonable grounds for knowing that he is not entitled to do so.

No further information is available.

End Notes

1   Parliamentary Affairs, vol. 47, no. 3, p. 354, Hansard Society for Parliamentary Government 2004.

2   The Guardian, 6 June 2003.

3   Latin America Weekly Report, 3 August 2004.

4   Roma, Ansa, English Media Service, 13 January 2004.

5   Hon. Lucien Lamoureux, Debates, 29 April 1971, p. 5737-58, Canada.

6   See Roman Civilization, Selected Readings, ed. by Naphtali Lewis and Meyer Reinhold, vol. 1, p. 132, Columbia University Press, 1990.

7   The Limits of Immunity, Principe and Practice, Department of Public Law, University of Vienna, Austria Today, 4/88/, p. 9.

8   David Beatty, Constitutional Law in Theory and Practice, University of Toronto Press, Toronto, Buffalo, London, 1995, p. 3. See the whole Chapter 1 for an excellent analysis.

9   Beatty, p. 4.

10   Beatty, p. 5.

11   Beatty, p. 5.

12   Hunter & Southam, (1984) I.S.C.R. 145 at 156, Canada.

13   A.V. Dicey, Introduction to the Study of the Law of the Constitution 1885.

14   On The Rule of Law, Politics, Theory. Brian Z. Tamanaha, 2004, p. 3,

15   Ibid, p. 4.

16   The Honourable Charles L. Dubin. Chief Justice of Ontario. <u>The Future of our Profession and of our Justice System</u>. Gazette, vol. XXVIII. 1994. The Law Society of Upper Canada.

17   <u>The History of Government from the Earliest Times</u>, vol. III, Empires, Monarchies, and the Modern State, by S.E. Finer, Oxford University Press, 1997, p. 1540.

18   Finer, p. 1540.

19   <u>Historical Studies of the English Parliament</u>, E.B. Fryde & Edward Miller, ed. 1970, Cambridge University Press, vol. I, p. 10.

20   May 21st ed. p. 74.

21   House of Lords (HL 105), (1985-86) p. 57, para. 6, U.K.

22   Josef Redlich, <u>the Procedure of the House of Commons, A Study of Its History and Present Form</u>, 1908, vol. III. p. 46.

23   G.H. Jennings, <u>Anecdotal History of the British Parliament from the earliest Period</u>, 4th ed., London, Horace Cox, 1899.

24   Hatsell, "<u>Precedents</u>", vol. I, 3rd. edn., pp 200 sqq; 4th edn, 205 sqq. 1818; Rothman Reprints Inc., N. J.

25   Conference of the Two Houses in 1641, May, 20 ed, p. 109.

26   Court of Appeal, Ontario, Canada, (1971), 23 D.L.R. (3d), 292 at 199.

27   Landers vs. Woodworth (1878) 2 S.C.R. 158 at 197-8.

28   Maingot, <u>Parliamentary Privilege in Canada</u>, 2ed, 1997, p. 26.

29   J.C. Holt, <u>Magna Carta</u>, 1965, p. 4.

30   <u>Historical Studies of the English Parliament</u>, vol. I, p. 75.

31   Wells, <u>The House of Lords from Saxon Wargods to a Modern Senate</u>, p. xiv.

32   Ibid, p. 262

33   Ibid, p. 263

34   Ibid, p. 264

35   The House of Lords in the Middle Ages, Enoch Powell and
     Keith Wallis, p. 1-3.

36   Wells, p. xix.

37   Philip C. Stenning, 1986, p. 17.

38   Crime and Punishment in 18th Century England, Frank
     McLynn, p.147.

39   Ibid., p. 141.

40   A History of English Law, Holdsworth, 1923, vol. 2, p. 128.

41   Historical Studies of the English Parliament. Fryde and Nutter,
     ed., Cambridge University Press, 1970, vol. 1, p. 168.

42   Brian Tierney, the Crisis of Church and State 1050-1300,
     University of Toronto Press, 1988, p. 16.

43   Western Society and the Church in the Middle Ages, 1970,
     Penquin Books, the History of the Church R.W. Southern,
     vol. 2, p. 102.

44   Southern, ibid., p. 111-13.

45   Southern, Ibid., p. 113.

46   Southern, Ibid., p. 117.

47   Southern, Ibid., p. 121.

48   Holt, Magna Carta, p. 24.

49   Ibid., p. 25.

50   Historical Studies of the English Parliament, E.B.Fryde and
     Edward Miller, p. 1307.

51   Mirabeau, Intervention à l'assemble nationale du 23 juin 1789,
     Hervé Issar, 20 Revue française de droit constitutionnel.
     1994, p. 675.Les parlementaires et la justice : la procédure de
     suspension de la détente, des mesures privatives or restrictive
     de liberté, et de la poursuite, Patrick Fraisseix, 39 Revue
     française de droit constitutionnel, 1999, p. 498.

52   Les parlementaires et la justice : la procédure de suspension
     de la détente, des mesures privatives or restrictive de liberté,
     et de la poursuite, Patrick Fraisseix, 39 Revue française de
     droit constitutionnel, 1999, p. 498.

53   See the excellent essays in The Permanent Revolution, edited
     by Geoffrey Best, Fontana Paperbacks, London, 1988.

54   Historical Studies of the English Parliament, vol. I, Origins to
     1399, E.B. Fryde, Cambridge University Press, 1970, p. 276-
     277.Issar, Ibid., p. 679, Revue française du droit constitutionel,
     1994, vol. 20.

55   Issar, Ibid., p. 679, Revue française du droit constitutionel,
     1994, vol. 20.Kopetski, Ibid., p. 11.

56   Kopetski, Ibid., p. 11.

57   PE 371.890V04-8.12, Report A6-0156/2006

58   Issar, Ibid., p. 689.

59   C.S. Franks, The Parliament of Canada, University of Toronto
     Press, 1984, p. 87

60   Herbert J. Schmandt and Paul G. Steinbicker, Fundamentals of
     Government, Bruce Publishing, Milwaukee, 1954, p. 392

61   See pages 7-8.

62   [1992] I S.C.R. 901 at p. 931.

63   The Times, 3 February, 2004.

64   Le Monde, February 2, 2004

65   Stenning, p. 291.

66   Parliamentary Affairs, vol. 57, no. 3, p. 564 © Hansard Society
     for Parliamentary Government 2004

67   Le Monde, February 2, 2004

68   Bratislava, 13 June, 2001, Ceska Tiskova Kancelar

69   See above, p. 27

70   See Globe and Mail, Toronto, October 25, 1990 (Geoffrey York): January 29, 1990 (Editorial).

71   March 29, 1994 (file number C16623), not reported

72   Regina v. Gabriel Fontaine, Quebec Court of Appeal, March 24, 1995, No. 200-10-000 49-949, not reported; Application for Leave to Appeal dismissed by the Supreme Court of Canada, September 7, 1995.

73   Regina v. Bruneau (1964) C.C.C. 1997

74   A.G. Ceylon vs. de Livera, (1963) AC, 103 at 120.

75   Albania, WMRC Daily Analysis, 9 November 2004

76   Brazil, Australian Broadcasting Corporation, August 12, 2009

77   Brazil, Associated Newspapers, August 12, 2009 NS

78   Globe and Mail Toronto, Feb. 4 2005 (Reuters); Geneva, February 7 2005, Reuters Ltd; Phnom Pen, 14 Feb. 2005, Reuters Ltd

79   (The Post/All Africa Global Media via COMTEX) December 01, 2004

80   17 February 2004, Latin American Caribebean and Central American Report

81   Santiago, Chile, 2 December 2004, EFE News Service

82   Chile, 24 March 2004, Latin News Daily

83   Beijing (AFX-Asia), 1 December 2003, Xinhua Financial Network (XFN) News

84   Globe and Mail, February 28, 2007, page A12, Geoffrey York

85   Prague, 18 February 2002, CTK

86   Prague, 22 February 2002, CTK

87   Prague, 6 August 2003, CTK

88   Prague, 1 October 2004, CTK

89   Prague AP, 28 January 2005

90   Ecuador, 10 Feb. 2005, Latin News Daily

91   Washington Post, 11 Feb. 2005

92   9 Dec 2004, European Voice, The Economist Newspaper

93   Fraisseix, p. 510-511

94   20 May 2004, Dario Thuburn WMRC Daily Analysis

95   24 April 2003, EFE News Services Guatemala

96   Central America, 24 February 2004, Latin America Weekly
     Report

97   10 Sept 2004 WMRC Daily Analysis, Guinea Bissau

98   6, 7 November 2001, Jerusalem, Agence France-Presse

99   The Jerusalem Post, 14 may 2003

100 Ibid

101 Ibid

102 Rome, 1 May 1993, The Globe and Mail, Reuters News
     Agency.

103 The Economist, 5/10/2003, Vol. 27, Issue 9323, p. 12, 2 p, 1 c

104 12 July 2002, Rome, ANSA – English News Service, by KSD

105 20 Jan 2003, ANSA – English News Service, by VB

106 Rome, 22 Jan 2003, Daily Telegraph, by Bruce Johnston

107 Rome, 6 June 2003, the Guardian, By Sophie Arie

108 Rome, 13 Jan 2004, ANSA English Media Service, by V.B.

109 Rome, 13 Jan 2004, ANSA English Media Service, by V.B.

110 Le Monde, 16 Jan 2004

111 Globe and Mail, Rome October 9, 2009

112 Latvijas as Avize, in Latvian, 7 June 2004, BBC Monitoring
     Former Soviet Union, June 2004

113   30 April 2004, AP Skopje

114   EFE Law Service, Mexico City, Sept 10, 2003

115   Globe & Mail, April 9, 2005

116   Mexico, 9 Nov 2004, Latin American Weekly Reports, Intelligence Research Limited

117   16 Feb 2004, Interfax News Service, Chisihau

118   Montenegro, 24 March 2004, BBC Monitoring European

119   19 Oct 2001, the Miami Herald

120   25 Jan 2005, WMRC Daily Analysis

121   9 Oct 2003 Agence France Press

122   31 Dec 2003, the Australian, 1 – All-round Country

123   Moscow 7 Oct 1995, The Globe & Mail

124   Moscow, 28 Nov 1998, The Globe & Mail

125   St. Petersburg, Russia, 14 Dec 1999, the Globe & Mail

126   Moscow, 20 Sept 2000, Reuters

127   Moscow, 20 Sept 2000, AP Dow Jones International News

128   Moscow, 30 Oct 2001, AFP

129   Moscow, 12 July 2001, AFP

130   Moscow, 31 Oct 2001, ITAR-TASS

131   Moscow, 1 Nov 2001, BBC, RIA-Nosti, correspondent, Irina Kolgina; Moscow, 1 Nov 2001, Reuters

132   Moscow, 21 Aug 2002, ITAR-TASS

133   Moscow, 26 Nov 2003, WPS (What the Papers Say) Russian Media Monitory Agency

134   17 March 2004, WMRC Daily Analysis, Dario Thuburn

135   10 Nov 2004, Interfax News Services, Moscow

136   10 Feb 2005, WMRC Daily Analysis, Christopher Melville

137 13 June 2001, CTK Business Laws, Bratislava

138 22 May 2003, CTK Daily Laws, Bratislava

139 28 Nov 2003, WMRS Daily Analysis, Mandy Kirby

140 Bratislava, 20 Jan 2005, TASR-Slovakia

141 10 February 2005, BBC Monitoring European

142 Linternationalmagazine.com. le 2009-04-17 UFC Togo

143 14 July 1997, Reuters, Ankara

144 19 Nov 2002, Globe and Mail, Istanbul, Tom Rachman AP

145 5 Sept 2003, Turkish Daily News, Ankara

146 4 Nov 2003, AFP, Sibel Utku, Ankara

147 8 Jan 2004, Turkish Daily Laws

148 Ankara, 25 Feb 2004, Economist Intelligence Unit – Rush Wire

149 12 Sept 2002, ITAR-Tass, English Ukraine

150 Ukraine, 6 Sept 2004, Ukraine News

151 20 Dec 2004, Financial Times, Kyiv

152 11 May 2004, BBC Monitoring Americas, El Nacional web site, Caracas in Spanish.

153 10 June 2004, BBC Monitoring Middle East

154 Belgrade, 10 April 2002, AP

155 Humanité, John Humphrey's Alternative Account of Human Rights by Clinton Timothy Curle, University of Toronto Press, 2007, p. 151

156 See Schmandt and Steinbicker, Fundamentals of Government, Bruce Publishing Co., Milwaukee, 1954, p. 132-133, ff.' Robert Nisbet, The Social Philosophers, Washington Square Press, 1982.

157 Quoted in Schmandt and Steinbicker, p. 133.

158 p. 138

159 Taken principally from <u>Constitutions of Countries of the World</u>, Oceana Publications, Dobbs Ferry, NY, USA.